CW01184086

Some Account of the Life and Character of the Late Thomas Bateman M.D.F.L.S. Physician to the Public Dispensary and to the Fever Institution in London
by Thomas Bateman

Copyright © 2019 by HardPress

Address:
HardPress
8345 NW 66TH ST #2561
MIAMI FL 33166-2626
USA
Email: info@hardpress.net

SOME ACCOUNT

OF THE

LIFE AND CHARACTER

OF THE LATE

THOMAS BATEMAN, M.D. F.L.S.

PHYSICIAN TO THE PUBLIC DISPENSARY, AND
TO THE FEVER INSTITUTION
IN LONDON.

" Multis ille bonis flebilis occidit."

SECOND EDITION.

LONDON:
PRINTED FOR
LONGMAN, REES, ORME, BROWN, AND GREEN,
PATERNOSTER-ROW.
1827.

LONDON:
Printed by A. & R. Spottiswoode,
New-Street-Square.

TO

THE BELOVED FAMILY

OF

THE SUBJECT OF THE FOLLOWING PAGES,

THEY ARE,

WITH CORDIAL RESPECT

AND AFFECTION,

INSCRIBED.

J. R.

JULY 2, 1826.

" Naturæ nostræ id quidem conjunctissimum est, ut de genere, ingenio, atque fortunis eorum, qui aut rebus publicis gestis, aut artibus excultis humano generi benefecerunt, minutissima quæque scire cupiamus; sive quod caritate quadam atque benevolentia devincti iis, qui de nobis bene meruere, eorum nihil a nobis alienum putemus ; sive quod in hac re commodum suum quisque respiciat. Cum enim ex clarissimorum virorum vitis discamus, quid naturæ, quid fortunæ, quid virtuti denique eorum tribuendum sit : ex iisdem etiam discimus, quid nobismet ipsis sperare liceat, quibusque rationibus id quod speremus consequamur.".

GUILIELMI HARVEII VITA :
Opera omnia a Collegio Medicorum Londinensi edita, 1766.

WORKS BY DR. BATEMAN.

1.
A PRACTICAL SYNOPSIS
OF
CUTANEOUS DISEASES,
ACCORDING TO THE
ARRANGEMENT OF DR. WILLAN,
Exhibiting a concise View of the Diagnostic Symptoms, and the Method of Treatment.
BY THOMAS BATEMAN, M.D. F.L.S.
Physician to the Public Dispensary, and to the Fever Institution.

In 8vo. (illustrated by a coloured Plate of the Eight Orders), The FIFTH EDITION. *Price* 12*s. boards.*

2.
DELINEATIONS
OF
THE CUTANEOUS DISEASES
COMPRISED IN THE
CLASSIFICATION OF THE LATE DR. WILLAN,
Including the greater Part of the Engravings of that Author, in an improved State, and completing the Series as intended to have been finished by him.
BY THOMAS BATEMAN, M.D. F.L.S.
Physician to the Public Dispensary, &c.

In One Volume 4to. with upwards of 70 coloured Plates. *Price* 12*l.* 12*s. boards.*

The Series of new Engravings, representing those Diseases which should have been figured in the subsequent Parts of Dr. WILLAN's unfinished Work, may be had by the Possessors of that Work, separate. *Price* 7*l. boards.*

REPORTS
ON
THE DISEASES OF LONDON,
AND
THE STATE OF THE WEATHER,
FROM 1804 to 1816;

INCLUDING

Practical Remarks on the Causes and Treatment of the former, and preceded by a historical View of the State of Health and Disease in the Metropolis in past Times; in which the Progress of the extraordinary Improvement in Salubrity which it has undergone, the Changes in the Character of the Seasons in this respect, and the Causes of these, are traced down to the present Period.

BY
THOMAS BATEMAN, M.D. F.L.S.

Physician to the Public Dispensary, and Consulting Physician to the Fever Institution in London.

8vo. Price 9s. boards.

A SUCCINCT ACCOUNT
OF
THE CONTAGIOUS FEVER
OF THIS COUNTRY,

Exemplified in the Epidemic which prevailed in the Metropolis in 1817 and 1818; with the appropriate Method of Treatment, as practised in the House of Recovery, and pointing out the Means of Prevention.

BY
THOMAS BATEMAN, M.D. F.L.S.

Physician to the Public Dispensary, and Consulting Physician to the Fever Institution in London, &c. &c.

8vo. Price 6s. boards.

LIFE AND CHARACTER

OF THE LATE

THOMAS BATEMAN, M.D. F.L.S.

Doctor Thomas Bateman, the subject of the following narrative, was born at Whitby, in Yorkshire, on the 29th of April, 1778, and died there on the 9th of April, 1821. He was a diligent school-boy; an indefatigable student; and an eminent physician; and left upon the minds of those who were familiarly acquainted with him strong impressions of the value of the habits which marked his character. It is not practicable to convey a complete idea of these to others; it cannot be done, indeed, in any case. But enough, perhaps, may be recorded to encourage both those who are teaching, and those who are learning, in the only paths which can conduct them to a successful issue of their labours. Examples of well-directed and persevering study, sound knowledge, and moral excellence, are not wanting to us, but they can never be superfluous. The more numerous they are, the more animating their influence; for the prize is not, as in other races, to one only who shall outstrip the rest, but to all who " strive lawfully." The more various, too, the roads by which it has been attained, the more reasonable the hope which may be cherished in any. Dispositions and intellectual qualities differ in every individual; their circumstances differ; different education, in some particulars, is almost as universal. Yet the field is open to all; and no honourable endeavours are quite without an honourable reward. The great principle, or rather the great duty, is indeed simply to cultivate the faculties; to make the most of time and opportunities. To begin with the beginning of these; and to be steady to the purpose, whatsoever measure of them may have been given, and howsoever they may vary, is the only sure way to true worth of character, and to usefulness. And thus it was that the subject of this memoir, although his course was arrested at the moment when each appeared to be arriving at its height, left behind him such solid evidences of both.

He was from infancy of a delicate constitution. His early childhood gave no indications of the ability which afterward distinguished him, for he was remarkably silent and reserved; and although always punctual in the performance of his tasks at school, so that his progress was sufficiently satisfactory to his master, yet he evinced no particular pleasure in the pursuit of knowledge, and never opened a book for his own amusement.

At four years of age he was placed as a day-scholar under the care of the Reverend THOMAS WATSON, a dissenting minister of learning and abilities, and an intimate friend of his father. At six he began to learn Latin; and as his habits of quiet obedience made him very exact in the performance of all which was required of him, his progress at school was considerable, and he was always at the head of the boys of his own age. With Mr. WATSON he remained seven years; and when eleven years old he was taken to spend the summer in the country, in the hope of more firmly re-establishing his health after the measles. There, having no school to attend, he became indolent, and gave up his books and tasks altogether. It was his constant practice to sit on the top of a gate near the house for great part of the day, lost in thought, without seeking either employment or amusement; so that his father (who was engaged in an extensive medical practice at WHITBY, and had little time to spend with his family,) used to lament continually to his mother, when he came and saw THOMAS on his old seat upon the gate, that "that boy would never be good for any thing."

In a little work of Mr. D'ISRAELI, entitled "An Essay on Literary Characters," it is remarked that this has been a very common prediction of the friends of such men in their childhood. If the fact be so, no small comfort may be taken by those who are apt to feel a similar discouragement in regard to their children or pupils; since it may justify hope under the most unpromising appearances, and support them through the task of still doing their own part; if, indeed, the recollection of that great duty be not of itself sufficient on the principle that duty is still duty under all circumstances, and that consequences belong to a higher disposal. The developement of the mind is, beside, but imperfectly understood. The late Admiral Sir HUGH PALLISER was wont to tell, that having taken the young JAMES COOK, afterward the celebrated circumnavigator, on board the *Eagle* frigate, which he then commanded, out of friendship for his family, and having made him one of his midshipmen, he appeared a very stupid boy, so that he had no expectation of any good from him. But some time afterward, in NORTH AMERICA, when the Admiral wished to ascertain the soundings in a difficult part of the great river ST. LAWRENCE, COOK, to his surprise, volunteered his services, and brought back his information in a manner which still more exceeded his expectations, and from that day broke forth with the talents which conducted him, in the end, to his illustrious place in the annals of his country. And most persons are acquainted with instances in which a similar issue has more or less conspicuously demonstrated the fallibility of the best and most affectionate judgment, and consequently the imprudence and danger of trusting to it, instead of persevering in the direct line of duty. Children of a shy and tender disposition are the more liable, for that reason, to be under-rated. Fearful of calling attention upon themselves, they not uncommonly contract a dull aspect and manner, while nothing can be more lively and sensitive than their whole frame of feeling. Disinclined to the ordinary versatility and boisterousness of their companions, as if they had been cast in the mould of those "whom," as Dr. JOHNSON said, "merriment confounds," they slide into corners and bye-paths, not because they love not their fellows, nor that they are without even a pungent sense of inferiority in many of the sports which they see gladdening all around them, but because for them, earnestly as they sigh for it, no fellowship is to be found:—

"Silent when glad; affectionate though shy,"

inconsiderate observers pass them by; or still

more unhappily join in the raillery which, of all things, disconcerts them the most. It is well if they be not now and then openly compared with some bold spirits, whose behaviour they know to be contrary to every lesson and every rule, and thus paralysed by the very stroke which was intended to rouse them, or driven by their misery into a forced imitation of what is most contradictory to their nature, and even to the instructions which are made a part of their daily business. A world of thought and sensibility is at work sometimes under such a countenance; and happy is it for the heart it belongs to that there is a tenderer care over it, still —

———— " provident of endless good,
By ways nor seen nor understood:"

and that thus the pain and the injury of unwise human management are counteracted, and over-ruled, perhaps, to some unknown advantage. Few endeavours are indeed more likely to fail of their object than those which are directed to the accomplishment of a change in the original character, apart from the implantation of moral principles. To make a shy boy bold, or a bold boy shy, is an attempt of great violence to nature, of very doubtful moral consequences, and, at best, an experiment altogether unnecessary, while there are situations to receive either, in endless variety, to meet the corresponding diversity of individual character. Rather than such an interference, such a departure from our daily practice of suiting the plant and the soil to each other, would it not save all parties incalculable discomfort to adapt the culture to the known qualities and bent of the mind; and to be content to prepare each, in such conformity as may be reached, to its own apparent leadings, so long as they are innocent; and thus to obey the great and benevolent purpose of Providence, to place each

———— " in the niche he was ordained to fill."

The opposite predictions to those just adverted to, are still more frequently proved to be erroneous. Nothing is more common than for boys to be held up as extraordinary for their cleverness. Yet, whether it be that they have been urged beyond their strength, and therefore drop their exertions as soon as they can; or out of their natural taste, and have consequently been disgusted; or that their vanity being excited, the thought of the notice taken of them, of itself enfeebles their powers, and, by secretly occupying so much of their attention, diminishes their efforts; or, whether the opinion formed concerning them has been altogether a mistake, certain it is that such boys do continually disappoint the expectations which have been entertained of them. And this error is a grievous one indeed. For there is not merely a falling short of the hopes which had been conceived, and perhaps blazoned wide around; but in this case the character is not seldom irretrievably injured. Instead of the modesty proper to such an age, little is to be seen but conceit and presumption, a condition perhaps almost the most hopeless which can happen to the intellectual faculties of youth, since it soon passes into an absolute effacement of that simplicity which lies at the root of every moral excellence; and precludes by its very nature all real desire for improvement. That industry, too, which is the only effectual mean of improvement, is no longer to be expected. For how can the boy be likely to bestir himself, whose head is filled with a notion, not only that he already knows more than his school-fellows, but that he also possesses a *genius*, a term with which he generally connects the fancy of learning without labour? So that, whilst in the end he is sure to know less than many of his companions, who without boasting or being boasted of, go steadily on with their duty, he is puffed up with more pride than the best of them. Whether, therefore, we think we see much or little in the talents of children, it would seem to be the part of discretion and wisdom to observe moderation in all we say of them, one way or the other; and, looking with a single eye to our own duty, only so to praise or to blame as may most strictly comport with the recollection that, of all our stewardship here, this account demands probably the most thoughtful procedure; inasmuch as its objects, so far as human means are concerned, are moved by our guidance, and upon us must rest the great responsibility of their steps being directed aright.

And, before proceeding to the subject of this memorial, it may not be unreasonable to remark, that in the day-school (as it is in the course of his history to speak of it), although of late years less thought of than it possibly once was, there is a moral advantage, for the loss of which few other situations can insure an equivalent. The affections, the precious affections, between parent and child, and between brother and sister, are not interrupted. The alternation of home and school is agreeable, of itself, to the active spirits of early life: and the intervals of study are spent under a superintendence, compared with which the public play-ground is indeed sometimes a fearful thing. Affection and principle are " pearls of great price." They may be preserved, it cannot be doubted that they often are preserved, abroad. But as the hours spent out of school are necessarily to be given chiefly to relaxation, and as this is hardly compatible with a very strict inspection by the same eye which exercises authority within, the vices so often lamented would seem to be so incidental to such a freedom of manners as to be guarded against only with the greatest difficulty. From the day-school, when circumstances favour that plan, after the master has performed his proper office of communicating his technical instructions, the scholar, instead of escaping to a licence, at the best, of use only to his spirits and his health, returns to a care for which there is a security no other obligation can provide; and for any defect in which, if it be not all which it ought to be, there is no excuse. Two objects are proposed in every system of education; the acquisition of knowledge, and the formation of the moral character. Both may be obtained at school. But there can be no comparison between the probabilities of their accomplishment, under even the most conscientious tutor that can be found (considering the unavoidable disadvantages under which his system is conducted), and under a conscientious tutor, and conscientious parents contributing their respective labours in concert.

During the summer which he spent in the country, Mr. WATSON had given up his school; and THOMAS was sent, being still in delicate health, to that gentleman's successor, the curate of the place, on his return to WHITBY for the winter. It was at this time that a circumstance occurred, which first roused his mind to that energy and activity which never afterwards forsook it. He was called up with a number of younger boys to spell English, and he felt this to be such a degradation to him, that he returned home, and with an animation and vehemence till then quite unusual to him, besought his father to send him from home to some school where he might have better opportunities of improvement. His importunities were for some time resisted; but as he persisted in them, and as it was also discovered from other quarters that he was right in his assertions of his new master's deficiency in classical learning, his parents at length gave way to his wishes, and he was placed in the school of the Reverend MICHAEL MACKERETH, a clergyman at THORNTON, a village twenty miles from WHITBY. The choice of this seminary was determined as much by the healthy situation of THORNTON, its vicinity to WHITBY, and the extreme attention of Mr. and Mrs. MACKERETH to the health and diet of their young charge, as by the abilities of the teachers, it being at that time a school of considerable repute in the neighbourhood.

Here, from the very first, he distinguished himself, and took the lead in every branch of learning, to which he devoted himself with an ardour altogether different from his former habits. Such, indeed, was his thirst for knowledge, that he joined sparingly in the active sports of his school-fellows, although he exceedingly enjoyed them, especially cricket. He pursued his studies, even in his hours of leisure; and almost his only relaxations were music, drawing, and botany.

The last-mentioned subject was favourable to his health, as it induced him to take exercise. He ranged the whole country for many miles round in search of plants; and before he left school had completed an extensive *Hortus siccus*. Astronomy and electricity were also among his favourite pursuits; and without having seen either a planetarium or an electrical machine, and with great disadvantage as to tools and materials, he made both, as well as an Æolian harp, from the descriptions in CHAMBERS' Dictionary, cutting all the wheels of the former with his penknife. His extraordinary diligence and industry, his docility, and his habits of punctual obedience, made him a great favourite with all his masters; and he was never once punished in all the years he was at school. Mr. MACKERETH was accustomed to observe, that his most remarkable faculty, as a school-boy, was his sound and penetrating judgment; and that he was not so much distinguished by quickness, as by the unceasing energy and vigour with which every power of his mind was kept in full and active employment, and brought to bear at once upon every object presented to it.

Many of his juvenile productions were preserved by that gentleman, and exhibited long afterward to his visitors: among these were poetic translations from the Greek and Latin; several themes, as they are called, written upon given subjects; and a few original stanzas of some humour, addressed to one of his companions on his want of taste and ear for music. His quick sense of the ludicrous supplied him, indeed, long after this period, with subjects for amusement both in prose and verse; and affords an agreeable example of that natural relief which is sometimes generated in the gravest minds to counterbalance their prevailing tendency; and which, as it springs up within themselves, and upon occasions which would produce no such effects in ordinary constitutions of intellect, provides far more effectually against the evils, if there be evils, in pursuits exclusively serious, than could be done by any extrinsic means. The ultimate source of such a quality lies, perhaps, in the quick perception of truth; in the habit of pursuing it into all its hiding-places; and in the hearty love of it.

To such a mind, a parody, however playful, is only another exhibition of the truth, either intended, or by some strange perversion confounded, in the original. And thus, it is probable, both the ardour with which he prosecuted his studies, and the readiness with which he seized upon objects of harmless pleasantry, opposite as those two dispositions might appear, were but different aspects of the same primary characteristic. Mr. MACKERETH's opinion coincides with this view. For judgment is but the discrimination of truth from error; and in all that his pupil either laboured at, or amused himself with, one and the same distinctive feature was prominent. There was in all, the earnest love of truth, and the unwearied pursuit of it. And it may be naturally imagined, that when truth, in its lighter and more enlivening forms, flashes unsought upon an understanding so skilled by practice to distinguish it, the delight must be in proportion.

At the age of fifteen he lost his father. His profession had been already determined by his own choice; but as no plan had been settled for his medical education, Doctor RAY BECKWITH, who had commenced his career at WHITBY, but was then a distinguished physician at YORK, was in the following year consulted on this subject.

By Dr. BECKWITH's advice he was immediately removed, being then sixteen, from THORNTON, and taken home to attend an apothecary's shop, in order to acquire a knowledge of pharmacy, while at the same time he continued his studies as a private pupil under his old master Mr. WATSON; and began also to learn the French language with M. RICHENET, an emigrant priest. Mr. WATSON kept him hard at work in mathematics, having a great predilection for that science himself, while his pupil had little or none; being used to say that it was the only study he ever pursued without pleasure. During the three years which he thus spent at WHITBY, dividing his time in the manner best calculated, as has been supposed by other good judges, for initiation into medical life, his only companions were Mr. WATSON, and Doctor ANDREW CRAWFORD, then practising there, and afterwards at WINCHESTER, who was very kind in his attentions to him. Along with these two gentlemen he commenced with great ardour the study of mineralogy, for which his native coast afforded a good field.

This preparatory education included all the great requisites to his destination. Without the early habits of obedience which have been noticed, a part of his childhood would have been spent to little purpose. But these habits made up, perhaps more than made up, for the want of interest and activity which for a time was observed in him. He went steadily on with his tasks, learned what he was required to learn; and so, little as such an effect was to have been expected, proved to be fully awake to the importance of having a teacher who could teach him. The incident of his urgency to be removed to a better school is remarkable. It shows how far the capacity and desire of improvement may exceed the thoughts of the most attentive and anxious parents; and may encourage them when they most despond. "*Lateat scintilla forsan!*" — and the moment may yet come which may strike the spark into a flame. In the mean time, *their* course is plain. For it is certain that their assiduities ought only to be the more strenuous in proportion as the child's own exertions are less. So that health be not hazarded, nor the powers of the mind overstrained, they cannot keep too closely to their own part. If this be persevered in, still seeing as the day comes, that the business of the day be done, their reward may be great when they least expect any. Circumstances, events, the situations from which the good they desire is to be educed, they can themselves neither foresee nor contrive. But these may, notwithstanding all appearances to the contrary, be ordered for them. Yet they may be ordered in vain, if that preparation which it belongs to the parent and tutor to look to, has been neglected or inadequately pressed. The soil ought, under any apprehension, to be made ready to receive the sun and the shower, or the pang, when they do come, will be far bitterer than that of mere disappointment.

But of all the essentials to the success of such a determination, the first is the habit of implicit obedience. Without this, little or nothing can be effected; with it, all may be done of which the character shall ever prove to have been capable. In the present case, implicit obedience was from infancy a principle. Whatsoever was directed was done because it was directed; and therefore it was only necessary to direct it, and to take the requisite care for due time and means. What endless conflicts,— how many bad passions are prevented by this simple observance of ancient discipline! And how much more effectually are the kind affections preserved, nay how certainly are they improved, by taking this rule instead of appealing to the reason of a child, or trusting to his will! Can it be too much to say how invaluable this habit must have been here? Desire of knowledge there was long no appearance of. Knowledge, notwithstanding, was added to knowledge. Time was not lost. And when the life and spirit required for its own propagation and growth were given, a sound and well constituted body of it was found waiting for them to animate.

The prevailing fashion, it must be owned, is not much in favour of this principle. But there is room to fear that it is so much the worse for learning as well as morals. Learning is not to be acquired without hard work; nor good manners without discipline: and neither of these is agreeable to the natural inclinations of youth. Are our youth, then, to judge for themselves?— The inexperienced to determine instead of the experienced? They in whom reason is only dawning, to choose before those in whom it is mature? Assuredly it was not in this way that the great characters of our country have been formed. They began, and they went on under rule; not disputing and rebelling at every step; but obeying, and that always: and by obeying it was, (be it remembered by those who dislike to obey,) that they became themselves "the master minds" of the world. So inexpressibly poor a thing in itself, and in its achievements, is pride! And so past all praise and all price a true humility! What an incalculable advantage have such scholars over all others, be their talents what they may! Instead of being preoccupied with the petty matters of their own devising, distracted by schemes of evasion, or fretted with impatience, their powers go undivided to their tasks, and they are accomplished almost without being felt to be tasks. A vast space of the blank, if, as LOCKE said, the infant mind be a blank, is as it were left free, which must otherwise be marked, perhaps indelibly, with characters of evil. And the spirits so dealt with are generally, as might be expected, stronger and happier. The ultimate difference to the intellect is of still more moment; and not to the individual only; for the effect of the opposite course may be traced in the superficial and arrogant language of much of our most popular literature.

But, above all, the mischief is to be dreaded in its consequences upon the morals and the heart. None, whether child or man, was ever injured by rendering " honour to whom honour is due." But the disregard to that command, and the contempt of the sentiment which accompanies it in an insubordinate disposition, pass by a natural affinity and progress to the pride which will abate nothing of its own claims, and presently spoils the fairest promise. It is impossible to perceive this result of modern indulgence without apprehension. A generation of youths soon becomes a generation of men; and although they may not improbably be vexed to find their own principles turning round upon them at their own firesides, it can hardly fail but themselves will exercise the same principles in their multifarious concerns among each other, and with society.

Already, in affairs not foreign to the life of a literary man, this reversal of order is felt in an assumption of authority which no long time ago could hardly have been apprehended to be possible. In those periodical publications, which exercise so material an influence over our literature, it is not rarely, it is said, that it is by far other than its greybeards that our opinions on the most interesting as well as the profoundest of human speculations are settled. They whose proper places would still be on the benches of the theatre, without ceremony walk forward and take the chair. They write what their elders, to the corners of three kingdoms, are to read. It is not within the present purpose to advert to this point, pregnant as it is with matter for serious reflection, farther than as it belongs to the subjects connected with such a narrative. The person here commemorated was in his youth an example of steady obedience: he exhibited its invaluable fruits in his modesty, especially, and his humility throughout his subsequent progress; and doubtless was the better for it even unto the end of his honourable career.

At nineteen he went to LONDON; and as will have appeared, well furnished with the knowledge, classical and natural, proper to his future profession, besides that which he had gained of itself in the course of the three preceding years. He was moreover, which was of far more importance, trained to habits of industry, and observation, and research, to a degree which proved in the sequel happily congenial with the turn of his mind to subjects of high practical value.

In the mean time his health had been much benefited by his residence at THORNTON, although it always retained its original delicacy. And, before entering upon the great change in his life which commenced with his departure for LONDON, it may be properly mentioned, as an instance of affection and filial attention not perhaps very common, that on his first leaving home, he asked his mother how often she would expect him to write to her. She replied, "Once a fortnight;" and from that time, through all the subsequent years of his absence, and in the midst of his most active engagements, he never in one instance exceeded the given period, even by a single day, the expected letter most frequently arriving two or three days within the time, closely filled with a minute detail of every thing which he thought would be interesting to his family in his studies and pursuits, and in the circumstances through which he was passing. He was so entirely separated from his family for many years, that, but for this correspondence, they would have felt themselves almost strangers to him. For the gradual influence of time, and circumstances, and companions, alters and modifies, more or less, every man's character. It was gratifying to them, therefore, to see the remarkable simplicity and sincerity which belonged to his nature remain unimpaired, much as he mixed with the world. This happiness might perhaps be more frequent than it is, if the first stages of education were conducted with more direct reference to it; if the affections were more cultivated, and watched, and cherished, instead of being left so much to themselves, and to the gradual corrosion of wrong tempers; if principle were made of the first account in conversation as well as practice; and the acquisition of knowledge were urged for its own sake, and not for that of exhibition or interest.

His correspondence, it may be here observed, was very characteristic of the prevailing features of his mind, always, as many valuable letters preserved by his friends might testify, expressing his feelings and opinions in honesty and simplicity. Letter-writing has in modern times been so multiplied, so much is written, and so much is expected to be written, that it might possibly be useful to many a juvenile hand if these pleasing productions of his pen could be made its models. Their excellence and their charm consisted in the absolute veracity to which he adhered in all he wrote, and in the unaffected language of every line. Having his thoughts always intent upon subjects of importance and real usefulness, his letters were substantial as well as interesting; in matters even of taste only bearing equally the stamp of sound judgment, and vigorous reflection. And he fell naturally into a just style of composition, not from studying any display, either of what he thought or knew, or of the manner in which he could exhibit it; but simply from his habitual love of truth and desire to set it forth. To avoid faults in expression, rather than to seek a fine phraseology, and to engage in no idle elaboration of unprofitable, still less of false sentiments, are the only secrets of good letter-writing; and considering how seriously the habit of writing well or ill in such a view, is connected with moral purity, or its contrary, to say nothing of the superior literary effect of epistles, which aim only to be faithful transcripts of the mind of the writer, the subject would seem to be of no mean importance to those who are concerned in the great business of education. There is a propriety belonging to it which cannot be violated without the hazard of injury to the integrity of character. " Hoc loco continetur id, quod dici " Latinè decorum potest; Græcè enim πρεπον di- " citur. Hujus vis ea est, ut ab honesto non " queat separari : nam et quod decet honestum " est, et quod honestum est decet."

Being intended to graduate at EDINBURGH, Mr. BATEMAN's chief objects in LONDON were anatomy, and the practice of physic. He entered therefore to the lectures at Windmill Street;

and as physician's pupil at St. George's Hospital for the winter of 1797-98.

Doctor BAILLIE, at that time in his best vigour of mind and body, and not yet engaged in very extensive business, both in his lectures and at the hospital —

> " Put so much of his heart into his act,
> That his example had a magnet's force!"

His manner of lecturing was indeed very particular. The patient gravity, and benevolent earnestness of his aspect; the simplicity of his language; and the conscientious fidelity of his whole mind to his office, were admirably calculated to fix the attention and attachment of such a scholar. No levity unworthy of his learning or his subject ever dishonoured either. The desire to teach, which animated his countenance and voice, if it did not actually enkindle, powerfully struck in with the desire to learn. And in those passages of his course, which brought with them the names of " the illustrious dead," as when he exhibited the labours of HALLER, or of WALTER; or was constrained to speak of his own great relatives, and predecessors in the same theatre, a tenderness was suddenly added to the dignity of their habitual expression, which, honest as it was irresistibly felt to be, touched his hearers at once to a right conception of the spirit, which raised those great men and himself to usefulness and fame. No man perhaps ever displayed the true professional character more completely than Dr. BAILLIE. None, therefore, was ever better fitted for the instruction of professional youth. An education as perfect as the earliest care and our best institutions could provide, sent him thoroughly learned in all the pre-requisites to accomplishment, into the schools of his peculiar study. His tutors there were of his own flesh and blood; and, gifted himself with talents of the first order, he was found equal at an age when so many are still idling, such had been their diligence and his own, to fill the chair of the HUNTERS. So well arranged, too, was his knowledge, so clear, and so ready his command of it, that he would say he could depend upon himself for a lecture off-hand, if awakened for such a purpose from his sleep.

In the abounding qualifications for public teaching with which our times and country are so richly besprinkled, this may possibly be a less singular prerogative than it might naturally sound in the ear of an admiring student. But if it be a common attainment, then may we rejoice the more in the privileges of those who wait upon the prelections of such men. For the value of such a mastery over subjects difficult enough in themselves is inestimably greater to the pupil than even to the professor, inasmuch as the perspicuity with which objects are seen by the former is of more account than the facility with which the latter exhibits them. The casual mention of such a power by Dr. BAILLIE lies in a still deeper remembrance; for it recalls, with the acknowledgment of whatsoever benefits belonged to the faculty itself, the sense of that entire veracity, and that utter simplicity, which made it impossible for the most heedless of his auditors not to admit absolutely every word he said; and interfused, with the affectionate attachment they carried far and wide away with them, a reverence for those cardinal virtues themselves, which could only be quite lost with the memory of his name.

It was said by a distinguished statesman of our own age, that the proper method of writing history was that of the ancient historians, whose aim was to " tell the story of those times." This simple idea sufficed to produce all the beauty and sublimity of their immortal works. As the story flowed, their language rose and fell with it; and, true to nature throughout, so the whole story was told. This was their object. The picture of their own clear minds was to be copied. The transcript, to answer its purpose, was to be such in reality. This singleness of purpose is the prime essential to every excellence: and this it was which made Dr. BAILLIE, as a lecturer and as a physician, so invaluable a model. This it is which propagates itself and its fruits, by an influence which no other character can reach. For such is the charm of truth and directness, that, combined with those qualities, sobriety, not to say severity, attracts and rivets far more effectually than any artifice of address, how well soever ordered. In this admirable man, there was apparently no thought but of the business in hand; and consequently there was less likely to be any other in those who listened to him. Nor was this the expression of a mind intent only upon the communication of knowledge. The enthusiasm of science naturally tends to inspire a similar temper around it; and very noble are the services to humanity which have been thus effected. But there is yet a higher frame. In Dr. BAILLIE, to the love of science was superadded a *moral* interest. It was hardly possible for the eye of an ingenuous student to await his respectful step from the museum to the table; to follow him for two hours, day after day, through his lucid demonstrations; still less to catch his kind familiarity, without this better impression of a sense of duty reaching his own heart.

Of all the departments of human employment, there is perhaps only one in which the formation of an appropriate moral character is of more moment than in the medical. And, to this end, the influence of the character attributed by the class to their teacher, and associated imperceptibly by his pupils with all their thoughts of him, is of the first importance. It is not sufficient that the qualifications of the Professor be of even first-rate excellence in regard to the subject which he expounds; although it be undeniable that this will be followed, not only by a proportionate popularity, but often by an enthusiastic admiration and attachment; and that under such a leader scholars of merited distinction will in turn be formed. These scholars are in a short time to take upon themselves the charge of attending the sick. And unless they go to this office with some sense of its serious responsibility, how much must be wanting, be that obvious or not, to its just performance! Although, therefore, nothing to this effect may be directly urged in the lecture-room, the impression made there may be deep enough to affect the whole course of life which commenced upon leaving it. For young men to think of their approaching profession only as the means of attaining to emolument or fame, may in some instances be sufficient to stimulate them to the requisite diligence; but unless there be implanted in their minds a sentiment in respect to their instructors of a higher nature than this; if they think wholly, or chiefly, of getting all the knowledge they can, without reference to the high moral objects for which it should be sought; the best of them may quit the schools with little else than their knowledge, and the fame and emolument which they reckon upon its winning for them, in their thoughts. To acquire insensibly, on the other hand, a respect, a reverence for the professional principle, will far more certainly insure activity and perseverance in study, and the necessary acquisitions for practice; and will place them afterward on ground at the same time inexpressibly more comfortable and more useful. These inestimable advantages demand no specific moral disquisitions in the theatre. A fit moral education being pre-supposed, they only need for their security that he who presides there should himself exhibit, like Dr. BAILLIE, the professional character in all his language and deportment: that he should come into it, and be heard of out of it, only as a man really in earnest to fit them as well as he is able, to do all the good to their fellow-creatures they possibly can. There is much in the world to be done, and to be done by them, if it be done at all. But it will be done as it ought to be only by those who set out with this principle, and who keep to it in all their difficulties. No pupil could honour such a preceptor more cordially nor with juster discrimination than Mr. BATEMAN. He was alive to all his merits; and made the most of them by unremitted attention. And none could be better qualified to apprehend and benefit by his best characteristics; among which that entire freedom from vanity, the noble superiority to it, so obvious in all the language, and in the whole deportment of Dr. BAILLIE, might well be impressed with peculiar advantage on a mind of so congenial a stamp. The modesty of the master's example, shining through powers so conspicuous, so adorned with all appropriate knowledge, and so earnestly exercised, confirmed the native modesty of the pupil. And as both were doubtless the more useful, as well as the more regarded, in their lives, for this invaluable quality, may the names of both, so widely looked up to by their contemporaries, and sure as they are of an honourable transmission to posterity, recommend it to all who shall profit by their labours, as a virtue without which the most propitious circumstances, the most ardent diligence, and the finest talents, even although these be all combined, must more or less fail of their proper and intended good both to the individual distinguished by them, and to the world!

The years of his studies in LONDON and EDINBURGH were spent, as they well may be by such students, very pleasantly. Studious indeed he was, and that always, and very methodically; but disposed by nature and by his previous acquirements to objects also of taste, and to elegant literature. So that his time was all fully occupied; and the evenings, which he delighted to pass with his friends, were chiefly spent in conversations suggested by the pursuits they had been engaged with in common through the day. And besides every other advantage, the attendance on Dr. BAILLIE's Lectures and hospital practice through a winter probably strengthened the bent of his talent for accurate observation, and of that character for taking practical views which he afterward displayed.

Thus prepared, he went to EDINBURGH in the autumn of 1798. His studies were continued throughout the whole of his course there with the greatest assiduity and attention. During the winter session of 1800—1801 he was the Clinical Clerk of Professor DUNCAN, Senior, at the Infirmary, and made the best use of his advantages in that valuable situation. And having been from the first a Member of the ROYAL MEDICAL SOCIETY, his time was again closely filled up. Nothing he had to do with was neglected or slurred over. He went not merely into the letter, but into the spirit of the institutions of that celebrated University; and drew from them, therefore, all the good they are so admirably calculated to yield, while he gained for himself a high rank among his fellow-students. He took an active share, as might be expected, in the pursuits and objects of the Royal Medical Society, and became one of its annual Presidents, an honourable office, his execution of which was distinguished for good sense, attention, and impartiality. At one of its meetings, he gave an instance of his habitual and paramount love of the truth, which it is pleasant to couple with a recollection of that instructive and interesting scene of inquiry and discussion. He happened to be in the chair when an erroneous hypothesis was adduced, and mainly supported by the ingenious reasonings of one of his personal and intimate friends. He was obviously uneasy, as the usage of the Society precluded the President from taking a part in the discussion, and after a time requested a member who was sitting near him to take the chair for him; and, thus joining the body of the Society, he by a copious induction of facts refuted his friend's argument: and, having successfully combated error, resumed his duty, as the President of the evening, " *Amicus Plato, sed magis amica Veritas !*"

"Quis desiderio sit pudor, aut modus
Tam chari capitis? ——

—— "Cui pudor, et justitiæ soror
Incorrupta fides, nudaque veritas,
Quando ullum invenient parem?"

He was a Member also of the NATURAL HISTORY SOCIETY; and in both, as well as in the private meetings held in his rooms for social intercourse, was much looked to for the instructive tendency of his observations, and regarded indeed by his companions and by the Professors with general estimation.

Mr. BATEMAN graduated in June, 1801, having taken for the subject of his Thesis *Hæmorrhœa Petcchialis*, and dedicated it to his valued preceptors the Reverend THOMAS WATSON, and the Reverend MICHAEL MACKERETH. He remarked, many years afterward, the turn of his mind to the investigation of diseases thus palpable to observation, which led him to take *Bronchocele* for one of his papers in the Medical Society; in this instance to the choice of *Hæmorrhœa*; and subsequently to the construction of his *Synopsis of Cutaneous Diseases*. He said, besides, that he had been often struck, while a student, with the general want of information concerning cutaneous diseases. It may be easily understood how much more agreeable the inquiry into diseases marked by external characters, than into any others, might become to such a mind, habitually fond of noting facts, and of collecting and arranging them. He would find in this path a satisfaction in kind like that he had enjoyed in his favourite science of natural history. And no doubt the love of truth, for which he was so remarkable, might, without any consciousness of such an influence, much contribute to the preference; since, so far as he could proceed, he would have demonstration, instead of reasoning or conjecture, to guide and be guided by.

His Thesis exhibits much discrimination; and contains a free but candid examination of the opinions of others. And it perhaps ought to be mentioned that it was entirely his own composition, some of the Professors condescending to compliment him upon it, and to express the pleasure it gave them to observe that he had written it himself; a gratification which their sagacity in distinguishing the style of a candidate, whatever be the absolute or comparative merits of its Latinity, may always enable them at once to bestow.

Dr. BATEMAN was now to enter upon a new and more important field. He had completed every part of his education with credit, and was provided with every preliminary to practice. His summers he had spent with his family in the country; and they were passed in the pursuit and enjoyment of those accessory accomplishments in knowledge, which are more ornamental to none than to the physician. To none perhaps are these indeed so useful; since, while they refresh his spirits, they enlarge his mind by information illustrative of all which peculiarly belongs to his profession, and qualify him for his rank; and thus add to his efficiency as well as his dignity. "Quæ quidem studia," says Sir GEORGE BAKER, "quamvis non faciant medicum, aptiorem tamen medicinæ faciunt." Without any direct view to such results, Dr. BATEMAN's habits, and the vivid pleasure which he received simply from the acquisition of knowledge, conducted him to them.

If it be true, as has been sometimes observed, that " men never rise so certainly as when they are unconscious whither they are tending," it is happy for the individual who has been thus carried forward, because he escapes in his progress the distractions and solicitudes, to say nothing of the still more uncomfortable feelings of rivalry and competition, which must always accompany a more specific pursuit of his object. It is with the studies of the lecture-room and the university as it is with the tasks of the school. One thing only is wanted, a direct and steady application of the mind to business, as it comes, without any thought of the ultimate consequences of mastering it. If these be let in, or if at least they gain any considerable hold of the attention, they must, in whatsoever proportion they may happen, detract from the sum of knowledge and advancement which would otherwise have been attained. The powers of the student ought to be, as much as possible, exclusively occupied on his proper subjects. To this end it comes to be of the more importance, that our institutions for the higher stages of education should be so ordered as to preclude, so far as may be, the operation of extrinsic motives. Can there be any difficulty in seeing how this is most likely to be effected? How do we proceed with the schoolboy? We do not set before him the advantages which he is to reap fifteen or twenty years hence in order to stimulate him to exertion. We do not tell him that if he be diligent he will be sure to be a rich, or a great, or a wise man. But we give him his work, and tell him he must do it; leaving his discovery of the benefits we are contriving for him to time, to others, and to himself; never dreaming but that among all these it will be made quite soon enough. We do our duty, which is to teach; and we expect him to do his, which is to learn. There is a season for all things. In due course, if both parties shall have been faithful to their requirements, will come another season. But if this be anticipated; if the mind fondly indulges in the imagination of the fruit, while it is yet only the seedtime, that very indulgence will dissipate the attention which requires to be concentrated, and thus even the very earnestness of the desire, and the endeavour after it, must tend to defeat its own object.

It would be curious to inquire what is, in point of fact, the ultimate effect of the high incitements to mental exertion which are offered in some public Seminaries : whether they do in the end produce the results they are intended for ? They are proposed with a view to stimulate the idle and the thoughtless ; and to urge to still greater efforts the industrious. And undoubtedly they do bring into the field a very ardent competition for honours. But does not a large proportion of the candidates stop at this point? They win, or they lose. What they struck at is hit, or is missed : and the fear is that, not having looked beyond this mark, there is then an end of all care of the matter. But the real object was to inspire a deeper feeling ; that, by means of this, science should be cultivated, explored, and completed ; and the power of usefulness to mankind as far as possible insured. Is this, the noblest purpose to which the intellect can be dedicated, to be looked for under such a system to any extent commensurate with its nature? Is not rather such a system at variance with the simplicity and modesty of science? And is the number of those who, having been disappointed in these contests, begin afresh, and of those who, having been successful, proceed, so great as to justify it? To mankind abroad these honours are nothing. The desideratum is the advancement of learning and science; and unless this appear to be promoted by them, they are of no account to the world, and may possibly do some harm to all the parties engaged in the arena. How analogous, rather how entirely the same, is the situation of the learner through all his stages from the beginning! Is it not one principle, that of duty, which belongs to them all? Is not every other motive, if not directly meretricious and mercenary, of doubtful quality, and still more doubtful efficiency? Once implant this, and fix it firmly, and nothing within reach of the mind can fail of being attained to. If, instead of the school-boy ceasing at his next steps to be governed by the constant reference of all he does to this great principle, *that it is his duty to do it*, he should still move under the same steady impulse and strength, how incalculably more easily and certainly would his ultimate object, of professional usefulness, be accomplished! Every hill would, indeed, still be a hill, and every mountain a mountain; but addressing himself in singleness of heart to each ascent as he arrived at it, all not absolutely insurmountable would thus be traversed almost without a thought of the pleasant land he was bound to, until his feet were safely at rest upon it. Is such a scheme of education visionary? The true way to determine such a question is to consider the progress of knowledge, and the actual methods of cultivating it. It is indisputable that a vast ardour in its cause prevails; and if its improvement be not in proportion to the multitude and the intensity employed upon it, it can hardly be unreasonable to inquire if there be not some defect in the manner in which the task is attempted. No one will say that there is not desire of money enough among us, ambition enough, love of science enough. Is it not possible, then, that there may be something else of which we have not yet enough;—that there may still be wanting that deeper and far more powerful principle which impelled HARVEY, and HALLER, and all other men who have been actuated by a strong sense of *moral* obligation; — a want which must be remedied before science is cultivated generally in the spirit in which it ought to be cultivated, and brought to the perfection which the necessities of human nature so plainly call for?

There is another and an opposite reflection which would seem to belong also to this view; that while it would best promote all sufficient exertions of the mind, it might repress any inordinate efforts. He who addresses himself to his labours on a serious and well-considered principle of duty, at the same time that he will strain every nerve for their accomplishment, and still think that he has fallen short, may yet recollect, that, as his powers are not unlimited, there is a point beyond which he ought not to presume upon them. He will remember that bricks are not demanded of him without straw. And, by thus keeping his endeavours within the bounds which have been appointed for them, he will, without danger of his faculties being either neglected or over-wrought, proceed steadily to the goal:

> "Est modus in rebus; sunt certi denique fines,
> Quos ultra citrave nequit consistere rectum!"

But if, on the other hand, urged by any other motive, be it apparently ever so honourable, he strive beyond the measure of his talents, how fearful is the peril, not of his failure of his mark merely, but of the irretrievable ruin of both body and mind! The history of students who have thus overdone themselves, and have fallen, never to be sufficiently lamented, sacrifices to their error, is very melancholy. And to theirs may be added the still more alarming examples of men who, in the highest departments of human affairs, have by an excessive urgency of their rare abilities, sunk suddenly to the most humiliating and most painful loss of them all.

It is true that neither the infirmity of our nature, nor the difficulty, in itself so great, of an exact government of the mind according to the scale of its powers, will admit of much confidence that such a stroke shall be by any discipline with certainty guarded against. It is incident chiefly to the most highly-gifted and most hopeful of our species, and among them to the choicest of that favoured number. But in proportion as the calamity more imminently threatens these superior spirits, how are we bound to watch over them, lest, by an unadvised flight beyond their strength, the precious promise of their course be extinguished for ever! Are we to stand still and admire only, as when a meteor is crossing our path? Ought we not rather to hail them as

"Lights of the world, and stars of human race!"

whose splendour has been given, not for a vain and transitory show, but an enduring benefit; and, in as much as in us lies, since its date at the longest can be but brief, to cherish and preserve it? There is one, and only one way, by which we can have any hope of effecting this; and that is by instilling the sentiment of *duty* with the first elements of instruction; by inculcating it the more earnestly at every subsequent step; and by recognising no other as legitimate through the whole sequence of life, from the earliest preparation for the race to its consummation. This simple principle, always readily apprehended, at all ages, and under all circumstances, equally fortifies against the two opposite evils to which youth is liable, that of idleness on the one hand, and ambition on the other. No elaborate representation of the consequences of either is required. All which is necessary is, first to inure the mind to simple obedience, and to refrain from the expression of all sentiments which can tend to excite in it the low feeling of competition; to set before the student a higher mark, which, without looking to what others are about, he can neither fail to see, nor can undervalue. In a few words, we ought always to speak and to act in his presence as moved and constrained by the expectation that he will learn all he can only in order to be as useful as he can. This is the only security. The faculties are to be kept in an efficient state for action. But this cannot be, if extraordinary efforts are to be sustained for an extraordinary length of time by extraordinary motives. No doubt a man, by the use of certain means, may succeed in his wager to walk or to ride from LONDON to YORK in astonishingly few hours. But when the feat is performed, his muscles demand a proportionate holiday; or the whip and spur must be urged even more violently than before, and presently his strength is exhausted, and the wonderment, as well as his usefulness, is over for ever.

Nor does the parallel quite end here. The whole matter lies, however, within a small compass. The human intellect is fitted to certain purposes. It is in vain to try to force it beyond them. It cannot be. Nature will have her due. If we are determined, nevertheless, to contend with her, to take no denial; nay, to withhold from her, when she most needs them, her very food and sleep, and to persist in our bidding that the very prime of our generation, after having been thus awhile —

"Shut from the common air, and common use
 Of their own limbs ——"

shall be devoted to a forlorn hope, the consequence must be taken with the daring, and few shall survive it. To the soldier, indeed, duty and honour are synonymous; and he who commands, and he who obeys, are equally without a choice in their extremity, and without blame in its issue. Come what may, their country crowns them both. Not so with the scholar. By a rash putting forth of *his* strength, the main end for which it was intrusted to him is defeated. Just as the scene of duty is opening upon him, he faints and sinks away from its call; and, instead of the imperishable honour of having added in his day to the knowledge, and thereby to the happiness of his fellow-creatures, his name vanishes in a breath raised for no advantage but his own.

The grand problem in education is to turn every power of the mind, without loss of time, to the best account; and again, remembering the brevity of life, to beware that we do not make it briefer. But if a temptation to overstep our narrow bounds should yet sometimes come across us, let us recollect the beautiful compensation which a diversity of talents supplies for their single and separate insufficiencies, and be reconciled to the unchangeable laws of our nature. "*England expects every man to do his duty!*"

Nothing could withstand the heart that conceived, and the hearts that stood to that matchless watchword! The principle is the same. "In hoc signo vinces!" Neither in that service in which the scholar has enrolled himself, may any do too little or too much. If he be either way disobedient to the rule, his rank is forfeited, and the most illustrious of all commonwealths is, so far as he is concerned, and by his fault, defrauded of her glory. In fine, let us be humble. There will be no excuse for us if we do not each perform our part. But it will be well to reflect withal, that the sublime scheme of human advancement, whatsoever certainty of instruments it may seem to imply, is altogether independent of our particular instrumentality for its completion.

In Dr. BATEMAN, nothing new, nothing of change, marked any portion of this part of his history. One and the same principle moved him throughout. In his childhood he had been remarkable chiefly for obedience; and his youth was passed in that corresponding exercise of his faculties which the sentiment of duty naturally leads to; so that he carried with him from the schools, one after another, all the benefits for which he was sent into them. He had wasted neither time nor money; had dissipated neither his health nor his talents; and so, with all the advantages which the best use of all these could give him, was ready for his vocation.

Before taking leave of this pleasant part of his life, a word may be pardoned, perhaps, in praise of the early love of nature (for very early may it indeed be implanted) for which he was so remarkable. With the facilities provided by so many valuable elementary books in natural history as are now to be found in all its branches, and the delight with which such knowledge is received, even by children, when judiciously communicated, the positive good which it must always bring with it ought not to be disregarded. A pebble, a shell, a flower, an insect, or a bird, there is no corner of the earth without. It is easy to deal familiarly with them all, and imperceptibly to imprint upon the memory — very wonderful being its capacity in the young — a world of pleasing facts, beautiful images, and

the sweetest moral sentiments. To whatsoever walk in life the youth may be destined, such attainments will be sure to be in unison with it, and to afford him a congenial satisfaction even to the end. For the often-quoted words of Cicero may be applied to them with a peculiar propriety:
" Hæc studia adolescentiam alunt, senectutem
" oblectant, secundas res ornant, adversis per-
" fugium ac solatium præbent, delectant domi,
" non impediunt foris, pernoctant nobiscum,
" peregrinantur, rusticantur !"

They have, also, if leave may be taken to pass at once to so homely a recommendation, the rare merit of being *cheap* pleasures, a consideration which Doctor AIKIN has with his usual soundness of judgment exhorted us to bear in mind when we are about to introduce to childhood and youth any thing to be so called. They fill up what without them and without amusement (for amusement cannot be continual) would be absolute vacuity, and therefore only an opportunity for the growth of evil. They, moreover, which is of no trivial account, awaken and prepare the taste, refine it from the vulgar to the elegant, and raise it from the frivolous to the intellectual : —

"Ingenuas didicisse fideliter artes
Emollit mores, nec sinit esse feros !"

If any taint be indelible, it is that of vulgarity. It infects the soonest and the deepest, and requires the most care for its exclusion. And where shall be found an antidote to the poison so effectual and so delightful, as in the garden and the field, on the rock or by the sea-shore? Whatever can directly or indirectly pre-occupy the mind with better thoughts and pursuits, whatever can raise it above the mean, and the selfish, and the common, all will contribute to future excellence. And surely it would not seldom be an inexpressible comfort that the entertainments of the youthful spirit should be of a kind equally compatible with solitude and companionship. The boy in a few years is to be no longer a boy, but a man; to confine the argument to its proper point here, a physician. And that he may be what a physician ought to be, the foundations cannot be laid too early or too carefully. He is to be taught all which is known concerning his art, or which he can, whether it be from the right or the left, turn to his purpose; and as a —

"Virtuous and faithful HEBERDEN, whose skill
Attempts no task it cannot well fulfil!"

he is to come to its exercise with "a pure heart, fervently," if he would accomplish justly all which belongs to his calling. This can only be expected when all the parts of his plan are consistent with its end; and assuredly they are all practicable. He not only may acquire a just and fine taste in regard to the works of nature, and a better judgment in manners and in morals; but unquestionably, if he be so happy as to possess these, will be in proportion respectable and useful; and, wheresoever his lot may be cast, his advantage will be conspicuous.

Dr. BATEMAN settled in LONDON for practice in 1801; and was admitted a Licentiate of the Royal College of Physicians in 1805. He carried forward his pursuit of improvement diligently there under Dr. WILLAN, whose high and merited reputation had induced many young physicians to enter as his pupils at the Public Dispensary. Dr. BATEMAN's assiduity at that institution led to his being appointed Assistant Physician under a tempory pressure of business ; and subsequently, on the resignation of Dr. DIMSDALE, to his becoming the colleague of Dr. WILLAN and Mr. PEARSON there in 1804. And he was elected Physician to the Fever Institution (the designation for the House of Recovery, or new Fever Hospital, which he always used,) also in the same year.

His ardour in these offices was unabated by any difficulties, so long as his health enabled him to discharge their duties. Those of the latter important charity were committed wholly to him ; and he sustained them for many years without any assistance.

It is difficult to convey a just representation of the earnestness with which he gave himself up to these duties, and to the farther pursuit of that knowledge which had already qualified him for them so well. But, in detailing the routine of a literary man's life, it may be important to mention his minute economy of time, because it was that, in conjunction with the unceasing activity of his mind, in which it originated, which enabled him to carry his researches to such an extent, and to provide that fund of learning he was at length in possession of. It would be hardly too much to say that he never wasted a minute. His pen was always in his hand the moment he came down stairs in the morning. His papers and books were on the table during the short interval which elapsed before he breakfasted. And again at dinner-time, the little space that intervened between his return home and his dinner being put upon the table, was employed in the same way, unless indeed it was given to the organ. For, much as he delighted in music, almost the only time which he spent on it was this little interval at dinner-time, and the somewhat longer one in the twilight of evening, which so generally passes unoccupied, but which he had been accustomed to employ in this manner from a schoolboy, always distinguishing it then by the term of *fiddling time*, because he could make no other use of it. In his daily rounds at the Dispensary he was equally careful not to waste time, taking every short cut, and not disdaining to contrive how to save even a few steps, since all these savings in the aggregate procured him a little more time.

He soon became a contributor to the diffusion of medical knowledge by his pen ; and, devoting more time proportionately to reading, his studies were always protracted beyond midnight, generally till two or three o'clock in the morning, and sometimes resorting even at these hours again to his organ, (and especially to the sacred pieces of HANDEL, in which he took great delight,) for the relief of the mental fatigue he so incurred.

His Dispensary Reports in the EDINBURGH Medical and Surgical Journal first introduced him to the public as a writer, for the distribution of an Inaugural Dissertation is of necessity very limited. To the establishment of that valuable periodical work by Dr. DUNCAN, junior, he gave very efficient support, being for some time its joint editor with that distinguished Professor, and the late excellent Dr. REEVE of NORWICH. Of the latter, his much-valued friend, he drew up an interesting biographical memoir, marked with great feeling, which was published in the eleventh volume. The eighth volume contains another of Dr. WILLAN from his hand. One of his earliest communications to the Journal was an account of the Fever Institution. And, besides various articles of criticism, Dr. BATEMAN was the author of an entertaining number of the Inquirer, in the fifth volume of the same work, on the connection between minute anatomy and medicine; and of some separate contributions, the titles of which its index will supply.

He wrote also the medical articles in Dr. REES's Cyclopædia, from the letter C inclusive, with the exception of that on the History of Medicine, which was furnished by another hand, during his absence from LONDON; and the medical portion of the article *Imagination* there, as well as most of the professional biographies.

Dr. BATEMAN wrote with great fluency. In writing for the Cyclopædia, he was in the habit of noting down on a scrap of paper the heads into which he thought of dividing his subject, then reading all the books upon it which he had occasion to consult, after which he arranged in his mind all he proposed to say, so that when he began to write he considered his labour done. He wrote, indeed, as fast as his pen could move, and with so little necessity of correction or interlineation, that his first copy always went to press. Neither was any part of this process hastily or inconsiderately performed. He said that, to prepare for the single article *Imagination*, just now adverted to, he read the greater part of one-and-twenty volumes.

It would be well if the same conscience were always made of such tasks. For in this instance, the conscience of fulfilling rightly a stipulated positive engagement, and that still more important tacit engagement which every author ought to consider himself under to the public, was his steady impulse and support. " The vocation of an author is a serious one," says Mrs. SCHIMMELPENNINCK, in the touching conclusion of her beautiful and edifying *Narrative of the Demolition of the Monastery of Port Royal Des Champs*, " serious, as it respects the writer, and as it respects the reader. That to which utterance has once been given, it is beyond the writer's power to recall; so that, in another sense, it may be truly said of literary crimes as of the sin of ESAU, that no place for repentance is to be found, though it be sought carefully, and with tears. The successful candidates for literary celebrity have a voice, which shall yet be heard when their place on earth shall know them no more; and which, like that of ABEL, though they were dead, should yet speak. Yea, and of every idle word which it *doth* speak, shall they give an account; nor can the united applauses of all men avail to screen them from the righteous judgment of God!"

There are more evils in the world of letters than criticism can control or even espy, if criticism were more just to its office than, busy as it is, we may boast it in our days to be. The multitude come to the perusal of a book, either as a meal they cannot do without, or as a banquet on which they are to feast. In both cases they are apt to take it as it is offered, without much thought of the manner in which its ingredients have been brought to their present shape. He, therefore, who takes upon him to provide for either the taste or the wants of the community, should bear in mind that he is answerable for all he sets forth. He is to nourish as well as to gratify those whom he feeds; and to make them healthy, he must look to it that nothing unsound or vitiated proceed from his hands. But the temptation to seek a little less perseveringly; to consider a little less carefully; may, in the obscurity and difficulty of recondite researches, not seldom be vehement. For, to cut the knot is easy; and the probability of the venture being discovered is almost none. The great master-check of religious and moral principle alone can save the writer and his reader from this noiseless wrong. The press is a vast engine. It is natural, in so just an admiration of its benefits, to think little of its mischiefs. Yet, the evil which it may work, by omission and by commission, is incalculable, when its true purposes are not recollected. The specific results of any given course of reading are very liable to be underrated. This is evident by the consequences which may be traced in conversation, in opinions, and in conduct. But, if they were of less amount than even is contended for by those who rate them at the lowest, the obligation to integrity is equally an obligation, and often, when least thought of, in reality most momentous. A title-page is a promissory note, and whosoever takes it has a right to the very letter of the bond. Before he sits down, it is fit, therefore, that an author should count the cost: for, if he undertake to instruct others, he has in the present state of knowledge to address himself to a toil which will call for his utmost patience, and industry, and self-denial; and which Dr. JOHNSON so feelingly in his own case compares with SCALIGER to " the labours of the anvil and the mine." Such a view of literary occupation, although it was suggested by the retrospect of no ordinary task, the very facility of composition attained to in modern times only makes the more striking, inasmuch as it carries along with it the obvious danger of our taking for substance what is nothing better than its shadow. The Englishman's noble old law of " *The truth, and nothing but the truth!*" is in no matters more imperative than in those of the press.

How many a vain hand would be put back to its proper distance by a timely recollection of that simple but comprehensive obligation!

During all the years which Dr. BATEMAN spent in laborious study, he never allowed himself to relax from it, excepting on those occasional indispositions by which he was actually unfitted for it. Society he was indeed fond of, and of its common amusements; and music he was fond of; and all these he enjoyed, as they came, with a peculiar vivacity and energy of enjoyment. But his studies never were intermitted voluntarily for any less grave occupation. Yet he seized his opportunities for lighter reading when they did so happen through indisposition, with avidity and delight; and often said it would be difficult for any one, who had not tried the experiment, to conceive what a luxury a poem or work of imagination proved to him after a long course of severe study. A delightful example both of the advantage of inspiring an early taste for such productions, since, without that, the enjoyment of them in after life is scarcely to be expected; and of their true use to men engaged in serious occupations. The relief they supply is not that of dissipation, but of refreshment; and they accordingly leave behind them an invigoration proportioned to their intrinsic worth, and renew the exhausted spirits for their ordinary affairs by an aliment, although finer and of more delicate quality, analogous to their proper food. The near affinity between the pursuits of natural history, and the objects of poetry and the fine arts, offers another invitation to the cultivation of a taste for them all in the first years of professional preparation. These interesting studies may be promoted best in concert; and much is it to be desired that they should go always hand in hand. To be well informed in the appearances and the works of nature, and to be initiated into habits of observation and reflection, are the chief pre-requisites to a just conception of the poetical character and of all kindred subjects. True poetry is but a simple, howsoever lofty, transcript of the sentiments and feelings of a powerful mind. It is not enough to constitute what is worthy to be so called, that a series of pictures be set before us, let these be never so exquisitely finished; nor that the most striking combinations of character or circumstances should be imagined. No doubt these may be rendered highly fascinating, and may charm away often a weary hour. And so may the Panorama, and many a show besides, beautiful each in its kind, and worthy of all its praise. Yet true poetry —

" Pure, gentle source of the high rapturous mood!"

although it summon every one of the senses to bear it witness, acknowledges not them for its source or seat, or authority. It is the language of a soul capable of holding " high converse" within itself. It is not the mere reflection of the images which have been carried into it from without, as by a mirror; nor, as in the kaleidoscope, a new arrangement of the elementary forms and colours which had been fortuitously cast together abroad, and there, as by magic, assume an order and a beauty which no other mechanism could have given them. We may be delighted, lawfully, with descriptions originating in these principles. But if, on account of the penury of language, we must denominate such descriptions poetry, we ought to discriminate between the productions which are in that sense poetical, and those more reflective and intellectual strains to which alone the title would have been given of old. The difference between them is akin to that which separates the chronicle from history. The one is involved in the other; but does not, and never can, constitute it, and bears little value but as subservient to a nobler purpose. We read HOMER and VIRGIL, and SHAKSPEARE and MILTON, for the sake, not so much of their wonderful powers of verse, or of description, or of their more wonderful insight into human character, and the world of nature around us. Unquestionably, they delineate the features of both, as no other uninspired mortals have done. But we hang over them, muse upon them, and quote them for their resplendent truth, and their profound wisdom, more than for their descriptions, inimitable as these are. It is not so much that we see better, as that we think better than we could have done without them. To the rest of mankind the universe has been comparatively a sealed volume. They have opened it for us, and, as we peruse it after familiarity with them, we —

"Find tongues in trees, books in the running brooks,
Sermons in stones, and good in every thing!"

The pre-eminent gifts of such poets as these shine only the brighter for the long ages through which, " few and far between," they have reached us. In proportion as they are more sublime, they insure, too, a more universal as well as a more lasting fame. For their sublimity is intimately connected with that capacity of sentiment and feeling which has been given bountifully to us all. The poet, who elaborates from his knowledge and study of a particular class of objects, if he choose well, and be fitly qualified for his undertaking, may construct a work of interest. But the interest is confined to those who happen to have a taste like his own, and those into whom he may have the good fortune to infuse it. Or if, through the force of his powers and his efforts, his performance catch a wider, nay the most just admiration, still the extent, like the origin, of such an interest must always be partial. He who travels far and near, that he may bring home something to astonish, may find, as all do who go on voyages of discovery, some unexpected land, and some undescribed tenants for it: and there are many to listen eagerly to his wonders. This class of poets may be compared to a tribe of musicians perambulating a foreign country with their strange instruments, each after his own fashion striking up a tune for such of the crowd as he can collect around him, the plaintive and the warlike, the tender and the gay, all finding their ample circles of hearers. They do not play in concert. They address themselves to a particular party respectively, who have no taste in common, and no sympathy but with their own band. But the music suffices for their object, which is only to be pleased. The tune is applauded. Its hour has passed; and the hand from which it fell is forgotten. The multitude care little for such poems; or, if they do rave about them for a time, they are forgotten ere long for ever. How should it be otherwise?

The whole matter on both sides is factitious. It is the *art* of poetry more than its genius that is here concerned; and whatsoever is so worked out must of necessity be liable to the imperfections of art. The garden and the park, delightful as they may be, are never by any contrivance or care made to equal the landscape. Nor does even Science venture to promise that the most successful analysis shall provide an equivalent for the simplest mineral spring. We may come near, apparently very near, to nature: still we do not quite reach her. Our best endeavours, indeed, are acceptable to a well-formed judgment only in proportion as they take her for a guide, and are found to approach her. But when we seem at last to have seized her, she wraps herself silently again in her clouds, and, transparent almost as they appear, is borne away from us with a majesty which declares her supremacy more indisputably than ever. In a word, it is not for us to *create*. What is called Invention in poetry is often but a torture of the fancy, a sort of waking dream, an extreme driving, " *vi et armis,*" of the whole available forces of the mind into array as they nightly and of themselves, —

"All huddling into phalanx,"

fill us with some strange amazement. But it is not every one who can attempt even this: and therefore, and because also the stranger the exhibition the more marvellous the talent, we confound it with poetry. The true poet writes, not because he is determined to make a poem, but because his observant eye and ear, always awake, whether he will or not, to external things, and his reflecting spirit, have accumulated within him a store of images and sentiments which, seeking with intense fervour for language wherewith to embody and clothe them, reaches it with difficulty. At length, yet to the last under an inseparable sense of its inadequacy to the task, such a Fancy —

"Scatters from her pictured urn
Thoughts that breathe, and words that burn!"

and charms mankind with a new aspect of nature. Every understanding and every heart bear testimony to its fidelity. As it is with Philosophy, so it is here. Expatiating in a wonderful scene, reflecting deeply, and feeling deeply, because he reflects more than other men on its phenomena, certain points present themselves to the contemplation of the poet, which, in a degree, shadow out something more than is commonly apprehended of man, and of what belongs to him as a moral being. Unobserved appearances of the inanimate visible universe, glimpses of human character, and intense re-action of his thoughts upon his own, combine for him a new world, in which he lives, as it were, a stranger among strangers, inasmuch as he continually feels the difficulty of conveying fully to those around him the sentiments and feelings which possess his whole soul. Still it is nothing more than a clearer and more enlarged view of things which he has obtained. It is not that he has conjured up, as in a dream, what does not or cannot actually exist. His thoughts and feelings are the reflections of realities, for which there is in his bosom a mirror ever bright and faithful. No impression is received there but he takes cognisance of it, cherishes it. It is food to him now; and he calls up, when he will, its affecting and beautiful images afterward; or by the power of association, they are re-excited by the countless occurrences of his life. The business of Philosophy is with naked uninspirited nature; of Poetry, with nature animated by an informing soul. To both, Truth is essential. If the philosopher wander aside from truth, we leave him to himself : and, in like manner, if the poet takes upon him to feign such a world, such characters, and such connections between them, as either do not exist, or are improbable, our interest in him is faint, or, if not faint, is but transitory. The foundation of all our interest, and the source of all our benefit, reside in the realities which in either case are brought to light. In each it is the reverent ministry to nature which alone achieves the wonder, and wins the fame. And hence the need of that rare devotedness and patience, as well as genius, in poetry also, without which true excellence is never expected in Science. In neither is this excellence to be attained by the painful extortion which an ordinary mind practises upon itself without mercy, under a perpetual dread of that oblivion which, strive as it will, must soon come; but only by that "intense labour" which MILTON said "he took to be *his* portion:" a steady, elevated application of the whole intellectual powers of a great mind to adequate objects, prompted and supported by an urgent and, as it were, illuminating sense of their sufficiency to the noblest undertakings. Notwithstanding the difference of their talents and objects, the same inalienable eye to nature is seen therefore in MILTON and in BACON, the same constant "girding up of the loins" to pursue and apprehend her, not under the charm only of that beauty which had been made so much more manifest to them than to others, but from a sense of the duty lying specially upon them to search out and declare her wonders; and, in their several ways, the precious truths shining unnoticed through her veil. The man who, in the cultivation of either, is intent on building up for himself a name, may not seldom attain it without this high frame. But even if it proved to be something more than a temporary illusion in regard to himself, it can be nothing better to his fellow-creatures. A story contrived ever so consistently, a fiction ever so ingenious, if it be not true to nature, presents to us nothing beyond the compass of the intellect by which it was formed. It may be indeed a convenient groundwork for the introduction of valuable sentiments and beautiful imagery; but the great end for which superior powers are fitted, is lost unless they are steadily fixed on the contemplation of nature in the external world, and of human character and events such as they actually exist, or have existed. It is only this employment of them which can lead on to the exalted privilege of lifting aside the mantle which hides so much power, and beauty, and sublimity from common eyes, although ever before them, and carrying them " home to every man's business and bosom." And it is thus only that extraordinary men rise to their proper height of supereminence, when our admiration of them rests mainly on an unquestionable conviction of their usefulness. For who will deny that in like manner as BACON and NEWTON are to be held for ever benefactors to mankind, such also have been MILTON and GRAY and COWPER, and as many other authors of " immortal verse" as have drawn their inspiration from the same inexhaustible source, and applied it to the same needful end, that of enlightening and instructing us. Their vocations differ but as those of servants of the same sovereign, labouring, in different paths, for the public good. They are unwearied, therefore, and they are humble; for the task they have taken upon them they see to be more than enough for the most splendid of their endowments. And the farther and more diligently they proceed in pursuit of that " *aliquid immensum infinitumque,*" which, like the Israelites' cloud by day, and pillar of fire by night, still " leads them on their way," the more perfect and unapproachable shine forth the purity and majesty of their subject. They are but interpreters of a language which addresses and solicits them on all sides; and which they would fain repeat to every ear as it has touched their own, and send into the depths of the souls of others as it has penetrated themselves. Whether voluminous, or known to us by only a few felicitous lines, their place in our remembrance is equally secure, for the stress of their hold lies in the happy discovery and application of the simple principles and feelings to which, when so exhibited, every human breast beats at once in unison. Such a seal from the hand of nature to the high calling, fixes the spirit, as it were by a bond, to transfer whithersoever it can its own " image and superscription," a service inconvertible to any other. But happen what will from it elsewhere, even though there be none to regard it, of itself it still testifies in its very substance to truth, and only with that can part with its character. The great predominant idea in such minds is the capacity of man for good. This is the clue, all but invisibly fine, which conducts them in their remotest excursions through the labyrinth, " the wilderness of this world." Therefore they elaborate nothing vicious, nothing sensual, nothing of folly; for in nature there is nothing of all these which may not be separated, and cleared away from their contaminating influences. They would have none to walk like the beasts that perish, with their eyes all their days prone to the earth; but would fain persuade all their kind to look up, with themselves, to the " starry threshold" of a better home.

It is our error often to misconceive the fine faculty we call imagination. For it can hardly be right to apply that term to any combination of phantasms which we may ourselves have put together, since these, having no foundation elsewhere, must always be liable to the same incongruity in respect to each other, and the same uncertainty of the consequences we make to depend upon them, as are found so commonly among the systems and hypotheses of pseudo-philosophers. Imagination may be not less a sober quality of the mind than any other; and a departure from its proprieties is often therefore as just a cause of offence as the more obvious absurdities incident to the understanding. For what is poetry but the mastery of that faculty of the mind which we so denominate imagination over the objects of taste, and affection, and moral sentiment, which a philosophical genius exercises over the elements of the material universe? To both truth is essential. The love of truth stimulates alike to the labours and the watches of both: the love of truth animates both to " cry aloud" in its praise; and so, if it be possible to persuade the world that in *truth* alone are its advantage and its happiness to be found. We refuse to entertain any other philosophy. We declare it at once to be illegitimate. Where is the authority, in reason or in experience, for any other poetry — if, at least, we profess to desire from poetry that benefit to the taste and the heart which we exact from philosophy for the intellect, and do not degrade it to the poor office of supplying a passing amusement? It is true that for such poets, as well as for such philosophers, we require minds of the very highest standard, as for the finest arts we expect the most delicate hands. " The description of Eden in the fourth book of the Paradise Lost," says the Adventurer, " and the battle of the angels in the sixth, are usually selected as the most striking examples of a florid and vigorous imagination: but it requires much greater strength of mind to form an assemblage of natural objects, and range them with propriety and beauty, than to bring together the greatest variety of the most splendid images, without any regard to their use or congruity; as in painting, he who, by the force of his imagination, can delineate a landscape, is deemed a greater master than he, who, by heaping rocks of coral upon tesselated pavements, can only make absurdity splendid, and dispose gaudy colours so as best to set off each other. Sapphire fountains, that, rolling over orient pearls, run nectar, roses without thorns, trees that bear fruit of vegetable gold, and that weep odorous gums and balms, are easily feigned; *but having no relative beauty as pictures of nature, nor any absolute excellence as derived from truth, they can only please those who, when they read, exercise no faculty but fancy, and admire because they do not think."*

But the question here is not whether, on account of the rarity of minds of so high a standard, we should submit to lower our demands, and be content with inferior performances; but whether, the facts being such as they are, we should not keep to the severity of principle, and admit as genuine those only which would stand its purest test? It cannot be a lawful argument that by proceeding thus we should at once extinguish a host of aspiring spirits, since a certain apparent measure of qualification is indispensable for admission to the competition of every race. The determination is a momentous one to both parties. For the ambitious, on the one side, it would be better that they turned their strength some other way, since but a partial and short-lived success can come of their most vehement exertions. And for the rest, how much would it conduce to their advancement in knowledge and taste and virtue, and in every quality which adorns the character and comforts the heart, if that large and important portion of our literature which belongs to the present subject could be reclaimed to the same ancient dominion of truth and simplicity, which holds now an undisputed sway over the scientific departments of letters!

It is difficult to refrain from a moment's glance into futurity. Who presumes to set bounds to the improvement of knowledge? Do we not, on the contrary, hail every new discovery as the harbinger of another, and a still more valuable; and anticipate a time, as well indeed we may be tempted to do, when, by the progress of philosophy, the conveniences of this globe shall be enlarged and enhanced to a degree of which we can at present form no conception? And shall we then venture to put limits to the expansion of those still finer faculties by which the moral world is illuminated? Why is poetry incapable of keeping pace with philosophy? Why rather, as truth in all which concerns us shall become more manifest, may not its sweet and solemn illustrations be made still more instrumental to the refinement of the mind, and the expansion of the far dearer charities of the heart? A sublime hope, not hastily to be deemed visionary, but only to be realised by the correspondent progress and freedom of truth in all with which we have to do.

Again, the unmitigable earnestness of the benevolent feelings seen in some few men can only be understood by referring it to the extraordinary power of the imagination. When they hear or read of misery, although it be as far from them as the poles lie asunder, and as unlike the forms in which they have been used to witness it as language can make intelligible, to them it is an actual presence, and they must perforce obey the impulse. Other men do kind acts when they see the tear and hear the cry of wretchedness; but for these, imagination supplies the place of the senses, and that so irresistibly, that there can be no peace for them until they reach, at any cost, the palpable scene of the affliction itself. And thus even the fact which has often been cited as a proof of the want of imagination in HOWARD was perhaps its very consequence; for how could he halt at Rome to look at the marble agony of LAOCOON, who was on his way to put an end to that with which he, as it were, saw flesh and blood writhing in TARTARY?

That the difference between such men and others, in regard to benevolence, arises in part from their larger imagination, is made farther probable by the peculiar calmness which characterises their proceedings. They would appear to act far more from strong moral principle than from feeling. They exhibit nothing like passion. What would have become of the sacred cause of the ABOLITION, as by a just pre-eminence it is styled, if WILBERFORCE or CLARKSON had been moved only by temperament? Many of us, it is to be hoped, might have rushed forward to the help of the slave if we had really seen him torn from his own shore, or set down in his desolation on another. But what we did not and could not see, they did. Their imaginations set him before them, and kept him before them. Their strong conceptions being such as they were, they could not refrain from doing what the rest of us might perhaps have done, had the misery been presented to our sight. And surely this view affords a far more hopeful prospect to humanity than any other explanation of the motives of those who so give themselves up to its service, inasmuch as principle may be more easily implanted than sensibility; and men are more likely to be brought to co-operate in "labours of love," when they shall have been convinced that they are duties, than while only their feelings are addressed. Principle, moreover, is wise and prudent: feeling is impetuous, and difficult of guidance and control. Principle is salutary, and strengthens whomsoever it possesses: feeling exhausts in proportion to its fervour. Principle must be the basis of a character " thoroughly furnished to all good works." The sensibilities with which our nature has been blessed may be more or less in different individuals, and no sin can be on that account imputable. But there is no abatement of principle to be pleaded beyond that which lies in the equitable comparison of our conduct with the measure of the light which has been vouchsafed to us: to that we are bound to act up. When they, therefore, whose peculiar frame of mind brings more readily upon their consciences the views by which great moral movements are suggested, prove faithful to the call of " the still, small voice" within, it behoves us to look well to their brighter lamp. We all can judge of its light, whether it be truly such as we ought to follow. And so may we all, whatsoever may have been the talent committed to us, alone discharge our own stewardship aright. We derive the twofold benefits from such examples, of learning from them views, and consequently principles, which might not have originated with ourselves; and then of witnessing their righteous perseverance in those principles " through evil report and good report." That they still suffer more than ordinary men from their sympathies, cannot be doubted, whatever weight may be given to the opinion that the main-spring of their exertions lies in principle rather than in feeling; because the former continually opens occasions for the latter, as it widens its operation in a thousand untold directions. But it is comfortable to believe that principle is their *chief* excitement to action, because principle is of better and safer propagation to others, and justifies our hope that they do not themselves endure that extreme distress from their feelings which we might at first sight apprehend. Throughout all things, so far as we are permitted to understand their constitution, order is a beautiful feature. The argument here fallen into grew out of an anxiety to represent the reasons for regarding feeling, however indispensable, and however lovely, as most subordinate to moral principle in the men who have been most justly celebrated for it; and for tracing it up to a stable faculty of the mind, rather than leaving it to its own independent vicissitudes.

Nor can such speculations be reasonably considered irrelevant to the matter in hand. The subject of this narrative found an inexpressible solace in poetry and other works of imagination; and it may be pardonable, therefore, in the remembrance of his labours, and the hope that others may continually arise to follow his valuable example, to inquire how the relief which their toils demand may, in regard to such gratifications, be best consulted: for to write a poem, and to conceive correctly of the poetical character, are very distinct matters; and what has been said of the one has been only for the sake of its connexion with the other. The old adage, "*Poeta nascitur, non fit,*" need neither be defended nor controverted for the present purpose, all which was intended being to exhibit the importance of certain views of polite literature in comparison with others, and especially to encourage its cultivation on such principles in those who are destined to the medical profession. Whatever belongs to that cultivation and exercise of imagination which conducts to clearer views of truth, and still more to the quick apprehension of human suffering, may well be recommended to every one of them. For who may with more propriety be brought by the charm of a right conception of the poetical character (or by whatsoever other means may be superadded to higher motives) to exclaim, " *Homo sum, et nihil humani alienum à me puto ?*" It has been said of Mr. JOHN HUNTER, that he had a great dislike to works of imagination, his long study of matters of fact having rendered every other species of writing disagreeable to him. The explanation is very sufficient while it is confined to compositions of absolute fiction; but if it were not presumptuous to remark upon such an anecdote, the very circumstance of that great man's exclusive occupation with facts, and consequent love of positive truth, is an argument for the particular direction of the poetical taste which has been here contended for; since it is plain that, despairing to find any thing like it in the works of imagination which fell in his way, he missed altogether the solace which, if otherwise constructed, they might have afforded him. And not only so, but, which was still more a misfortune, he missed the benefit which invariably attends the discovery of that beautiful analogy which runs through all the forms of truth, like the link which binds together our kindred, and may be recognised in the most distant. This pleasant aid to the spirits and the strength can come, indeed, but seldom, and in very stinted portions, to those who are engaged in laborious researches, for the lot of man allows of but little deviation from his path; yet, as there must needs be some refreshment by the way, it is the part of wisdom to provide such as, with the cordial, brings substantial replenishment: or, if this be thought too strict a rule, that at least the cup be unvitiated.

No reader was ever better qualified than Dr. BATEMAN to enjoy the moments which could be snatched for such books as administer delight to a pure and cultivated taste. He had grown up in the love of nature, and his early scientific pursuits had helped to confirm it into a habit. A sound classical scholar, too, he came to the perusal of a poem, or any other production of the "*literæ humaniores*," with the sufficiency of a critic; and might naturally therefore fly to them as he did in weariness and in sickness. Yet they never encroached an instant, it may be safely affirmed, on the duties he had prescribed to himself, notwithstanding this keen sense of their charm. The time belonging to those higher avocations, howsoever secure from all human cognisance, he gave them to the full. His other readings served as a congenial relief to a frame unconsciously wearing down by mental occupation; and, no doubt, so much the more effectually, because none but an uncorrupt taste could gratify his own, prepared as it was by education, as well as by native disposition, to turn instinctively from every other; for the solace of such reading can be only in proportion to its purity, and to the just measure which it is made to keep to every serious requirement. He did but carry, indeed, the same energy of mind and feeling into these particular seasons which accompanied all that he did, and all that he enjoyed. Yet, with a sensibility exceedingly acute, and with warm affections, the extreme reserve of his character prevented almost all expression of his feelings, and gave a coldness to his manner very foreign to the true state of them. For whatever value he might have observed to be given to any supposed standard of manners, it was at no part of his life an object with him to mould himself according to it. Sincere, and of an integrity which became so much a part of his nature, that its expression was, as it were, without consideration or consciousness, his language was simple and direct, and his whole deportment plain, and without pretension. In small matters and in great his regard to truth was strict and direct; in proof of which it can hardly be amiss to mention an instance of it which occurred when he was once at Harrogate. On going out from his lodgings to an evening party, he had told his landlady that he would be back at a particular hour. He was pressed, however, to stay longer, and the company being agreeable, a friend on returning with him expressed some regret that he had not given way to the invitation, as he would have liked to remain. " So should I too," said Dr. BATEMAN ; " but I had said that I would be at home at twelve o'clock, and I could not break my word, if it were to a chambermaid."

His mind and his heart were too full of their proper business for any concern about smaller matters ; a happy proof, if any were needed, of the sufficiency of ability and knowledge in his profession to success. Would that the example might move to a similar earnestness in study and in practice, wheresoever it is for a moment relaxed by an unworthy solicitude about exterior recommendations ! There is only one proper object for the physician to set before him ; and that is a great and very serious one, — to learn all he can, and to do all he can, for the good and the comfort of the sick and the miserable. This is quite enough for his attention ; and whatever contributes directly or indirectly to this accomplishment, it will be inexpressibly a satisfaction to him to have striven for with all his might and all his strength. For the rest, it is better left; and when left, for his encouragement he may be assured it is better adjusted.

In private practice, as well as in the public institutions with which he was connected, Dr. BATEMAN's conduct was uniformly deserving of praise. The motto of his family bearings, "*Nec prece nec pretio,*" was remarkably characteristic of the temper of his mind. Neither entreaty nor interest could ever have withdrawn him from the path of his duty. This firmness of purpose is especially important to the medical character; and being tempered in Dr. BATEMAN by good sense and a kindly disposition, it acquired for him a proportionate weight in the estimation of his professional brethren.

With all his laborious exertions, his advance to the more profitable employments of his profession was slow, as will generally be the case under the circumstances of talent, however strong and persevering, making its own unassisted way. On Dr. WILLAN's regretted illness, and consequent departure to Madeira in 1811, Dr. BATEMAN became the principal authority on all questions relating to affections of the skin. In this department his practice was progressively productive of more emolument, whilst by the confidence reposed in his ability and integrity by his professional friends, and the medical world at large, it was becoming more and more extended in its general reputation. And his distinction as an author, and a skilful practitioner in cutaneous diseases, was well confirmed by the appearance of his SYNOPSIS in 1813.

His views and conduct in the publication of this valuable work he has given in a clear and explicit statement in the preface; in which his respect and regard for the memory and fame of Dr. WILLAN were evinced, as well as in the friendly and able biographical memoir which has been already mentioned. The Synopsis was followed by his *Delineations*. Although by diligence in studying the definitions of the generic and specific distinctions in the forms of cutaneous affections, through the accuracy of the descriptive language which Dr. BATEMAN, following the example of Dr. WILLAN, was careful to employ, a sufficiently correct and discriminative knowledge of them may undoubtedly be acquired, yet this latter work must be regarded as one of essential importance in facilitating the acquisition of a ready diagnostic tact. The plates are in part those of Dr. WILLAN, retouched and improved by the engraver, and partly original. Several characteristic representations among them are from Dr. BATEMAN's own pencil. His early observation of the general deficiency of information on the subject of this important class of diseases remained on his mind when he came to settle in LONDON. And he there happily fell into that acquaintance with Dr. WILLAN, which at the same time fostered and facilitated his own particular turn to such researches, and conducted him in the end to a knowledge in them of which the least that can be said will be that it justly entitled him to an eminence no one had enjoyed before in that department of practice. The best test of medical excellence is the general confidence of the medical world itself. This testimony was amply borne to the merits of Dr. BATEMAN, few practitioners of his years having perhaps been regarded with more.

In the present state of EUROPE a name, howsoever gained, travels fast. And if this sometimes happen to such as little merit distinction, the wider the mistake, the sooner probably may it be discovered; and the mischief, if any have been done, may be more certainly repaired. In such instances as that here recorded, the advantage of rapid and extended communication is inestimable. Improvement in knowledge can no where be superfluous; and the earnestness as well as the number of its enlightened cultivators through the civilised world is increased by the intelligence of any success in any part of it. The Synopsis was soon translated into the French, German, and Italian languages. And if it be always right to render " honour to whom honour" is due, it would be unjust not to mention a pleasing instance of regard to science and humanity with which Dr. BATEMAN was about this time gratified from a very high quarter. The EMPEROR OF RUSSIA was pleased to desire, by a letter written by his own physician to Dr.

BATEMAN, that copies of his books might be sent to him through the hands of the Imperial Ambassador in LONDON. And on the command being carefully fulfilled, HIS MAJESTY farther condescended to convey to him, by the same distinguished channel, a ring of a hundred guineas' value, with a gracious intimation of the Imperial pleasure that any future works written by Dr. BATEMAN should be transmitted in like manner to ST. PETERSBURGH.

Amidst his various labours, Dr. BATEMAN's health, which had been originally so delicate, began to give way. To derangement of the functions of the digestive organs, and successive attacks of periodic head-ach, was superadded a gradual failure of the sight of his right eye, which was considered to be of the nature of *amaurosis*. And as the vision in the left eye was also to a certain degree affected, it was resolved to have recourse to mercury. And the condition of his general health as well as that of the digestive organs, having been improved by a residence of several weeks at the sea-side, this plan was commenced early in the year 1817.

But it soon proved necessary to forego its farther prosecution, on account of the distressing train of symptoms which ensued, and of which he published himself a very interesting sketch in the ninth volume of the Medico-Chirurgical Transactions. These symptoms were clearly to be referred to that state of the system so ably described as the mercurial erethism by Mr. PEARSON, to whom the profession of medicine is deeply indebted for having pointed out that particular morbid influence which not very unfrequently attends the constitutional excitement produced by this mineral; and which, when overlooked, has sometimes led to fatal consequences. Dr. BATEMAN often dwelt afterward on his recovery from the alarming situation to which he had been reduced at this time, with particular warmth of feeling, always eager in his attention to direct practical facts in the treatment of dangerous maladies; and on this occasion owing, as he believed, so much personally to the sagacity and decision of the eminent man with whom it had so long been his happiness to act in concert at the Public Dispensary. He entertained, indeed, for Mr. PEARSON an unfeigned respect, and at all times gladly listened to his opinions in the expectation of information and instruction upon which he might depend. For he knew how to appreciate the profound erudition, the philosophical severity of judgment, and the rare integrity which have marked the noiseless and unostentatious character of that excellent surgeon throughout his long and laborious course. "*Laudari à laudato viro*" has been held from of old to be the soundest testimony to worth, and in the present case it may claim the value, if indeed human praise to such a mind have any value, of a homage in some sense sacred now that it can only be offered from the tomb. And let us be pardoned, in the moment of regret for the early disappearance of one bright example of professional usefulness from a scene where it is so much needed, for a natural anxiety to render a rightful tribute also to such as we may yet be permitted to hope for good from. For the rich stores of so many years' painful study, of so absolute a dedication of all the intellectual powers to the acquisition of knowledge, of such an exemplary obedience to the strictest rules of investigation and reasoning, cannot be known without a fervent desire for their farther and more durable application to the common advancement of science and sound learning. Still less can the experience of essential benefits, conferred in the utmost simplicity and patience of disinterested benevolence, be remembered without a wish that the Christian principles from which it flowed could likewise be recommended by a hand so familiar with whatever is useful or attractive in ancient and modern letters, and a judgment in the best of all truth so complete! *

The illness with which Dr. BATEMAN had been first rather suddenly attacked in the spring of 1815 left effects from which he never recovered. He suspected at the time, from the very

* How has the death of this venerable man at the moment of these sheets being sent to the press quickened every affectionate and reverent thought of him, and what a relief would it now be, if this were the time or place for it, to bear still farther testimony to his manifold endowments and exalted character!

severe pain he suffered in the lower part of the left side of the back, (which no means employed either removed or alleviated for some weeks,) that there must be some organic disease; and it was not until he had been examined by Dr. BAILLIE that he could be persuaded the disorder was only functional. From that time, however, he enjoyed no more good health, having feverish nights, and more or less of a distressing flatulent cough, these being much aggravated by every additional bodily exertion. Hence his journeys into the north, which he took more frequently in the hope of reaping the same benefit from them as formerly, now invariably increased his feverishness and debility.

These journeys had been indeed as delightful to him as they were useful. For he enjoyed, on such occasions, as much perhaps as man could enjoy them, the affectionate intercourse with his family, which was their main object; and the opportunities which he sometimes took with them of some interesting farther excursion. In a letter written soon after his return to LONDON from one of the earliest of these visits, he says, " During my three months' sojourning in the country, I effected, what I have long enjoyed in anticipation, though almost without hope, a ramble through CUMBERLAND and WESTMORELAND. After riding about 110 miles, I met two friends from LONDON, at KENDAL. We traversed all the sublime and interesting routes, which travellers usually pursue in those charming counties, and saw two lakes, in addition to those which are commonly visited. We were but a week among those enchanting scenes; but it was a week of uninterrupted enjoyment; every minute that could be spared from sleep and hasty meals was spent in the active pursuit of those objects of admiration which abound in all directions. We were extremely fortunate, too, in the weather, which combined in general with the characteristic features of the landscape to produce that unity and harmony of the whole scene which is so seldom found in nature, and which it is the perfection of art to produce and apply. We viewed ULLSWATER, for example, (perhaps the most beautiful and interesting of the lakes,) which is marked by a striking union of sublimity and beauty, placid, yet grand; sufficiently adorned to allure the eye, yet bold enough in its features to elevate the mind to solemn admiration. This scene we enjoyed on the bosom of the lake, while the moon " in clouded majesty arose," and alternately broke forth in splendour, and again was hid in obscurity. And to this must be added, that the huntsman's bugle-horn was sounding at intervals, and echoing among the mountains. The scene accorded in all its parts, and impressed us with sensations, the remembrance of which will not very soon be effaced. To the frowning grandeur of DERWENT-WATER, at KESWICK, we first approached in a grey evening, when the clouds were louring on the mountain tops, and shed a gloom, which, by harmonising with the character of the scene, wonderfully heightened the effect of the first impression. And we first saw the calm and far-spreading WINDERMERE at noon, under a bright and almost cloudless sky; forming a landscape which the pencil of CLAUDE LORRAINE might have copied, without the addition or abstraction of one feature to improve the unity of expression which is so essential to the full excitement of the emotions of taste :

> "' Hic gelidi fontes; hic mollia prata, Lycori;
> Hic nemus; hic ipso tecum consumerer ævo !' "

Whether in town, indeed, or in country, his sensibility turned, with a happy sense of the relief they were adapted to yield him, to the beauties which a well cultivated taste may find in either. " I have been looking," he writes in another letter, " into one or two of our older poets, who in general do not stand in very high estimation, principally from the recommendation of Dr. DRAKE, in his ' Literary Hours.' And I have been highly pleased with BEAUMONT and FLETCHER's ' Faithful Shepherdess,' which is on the whole a charming pastoral, in the true Theocritan style of simplicity, bating, however, a little of the licentious turn and expression, which are to be attributed perhaps solely to the *age* they wrote in. This description of an autumnal morning is, I think, hardly to be excelled : —

"'See, the day begins to break,
And the light shoots like a streak
Of subtile fire; the wind blows cold,
While the morning doth unfold;
Now the birds begin to rouse,
And the squirrel from the boughs
Leaps, to get him nuts and fruit;
The early lark, that erst was mute,
Carols to the rising day
Many a note, and many a lay.'

"Or this little passage:—

"'The nightingale, among the thick-leaved spring
That sits alone in sorrow and doth sing
Whole nights away in mourning; or the owl;
Or our great enemy, that still doth howl
Against the moon's cold beams.'"

Who would not sympathise with the man, who could so enjoy the solace which such walks and rides, and such readings, alternately supplied! Who would not wish that they might have been more, and his labours less! "I feel my avocations crowd upon me," says a third letter, "and time appears short, when I look forward, and consider the literary and medical occupations of the winter; Cyclopædia, Register, Journal, besides professional duties, seem to be capable of filling up more time than lies before me. And like every dyspeptic man, I cannot command my exertions: when I can employ them, I generally feel that my literary engagements are pressing upon me, and that they must be attended to: writing, therefore, is my labour; and with the exception, therefore, of writing to my mother (which I do regularly as a paramount duty), I must submit to the imputation of unkindness by an irregular, and sometimes an almost suspended correspondence. But I wish you to believe that such is not the state of my mind." Yet, in the midst of his engagements and duties, he was remarkable always for order and method. Without these habits, indeed, the accumulation of business, of whatsoever kind, seldom leads to much real usefulness: with them, the amount of that which may be effected is often in such instances surprising. His handwriting was very plain; he was fond of arrangement and classification; and his distribution of employment was regular; and all these contributed to the satisfactory dispatch of the obligations of each day as it came, and not unfrequently facilitated future tasks, as well as suggested sources of innocent amusement. His commonplace books contain valuable examples of both ; of the application of that well-practised " *lucidus ordo*" to a great variety of subjects in turn, from the definitions of nosology, to the origins of surnames ; and throughout exhibit very strikingly a constant observation of facts, and of whatever was curious or useful wheresoever he met with it. Whether some parts of these books, which belong to medicine, may not yet be separated, and so made serviceable to the public, it is much a duty to consider. In the mean time, the following " Queries," copied out of them, from a long series of different heads, may show the general frame and activity of his mind : —

" Are not *moral feelings* and a *taste* for literature and the fine arts closely connected in our nature ?

" To what extent does our connate *sense of beauty* and the faculty of *association* respectively operate in exciting emotions of taste ?

" Is there not a considerable difference between the faculties of *associating ideas* with *ideas*, and *ideas* with *impressions*, both of which are usually comprehended under the term *association ?*

" Is *prejudice* always to be held in contempt, and annihilated where it is possible? Does it not contribute much to our *pleasures* in matters of taste; to our *happiness* in theological matters; to our *power* in political; to our *moral bonds* in civil society? And are not the wisest of mankind swayed by it unalterably in innumerable ways?— Understanding by *prejudice* every sentiment not deduced by the individual from comparing the arguments on which it is founded.

" Does our pleasure in contemplating the excellencies of nature and art increase in a ratio proportionate to the increase of our taste?

" Is it probable that Physiognomy can ever be reduced to a science?

" Do we not put a false estimate on the *vices* of men by associating them with the *punishments* denounced against them by undiscriminating legislators rather than measuring their atrocity by its true standard, — the effects on our fellow-creatures? Is stealing sixpence worthy of death, and ruining female honour and peace an honourable levity?

" And do we not estimate falsely the *productions of Genius*, when we are dazzled by the extent or novelty of the *intellectual exertion*, and overlook the *utility* of it, or its influence on our well-being and happiness? Is the discovery of the Georgium Sidus, and the calculation of its orbit, a sublime and meritorious act of science; and shall we silently receive light from Argand's lamp or drink from the potter's mug, without reflecting that thousands receive some addition to their comforts from the latter?

" Is the common opinion correct, that *Genius* is *shackled* by the *rules* of criticism? and that Shakspeare, for example, would probably not have displayed those transcendent beauties of his muse, if he had known and confined himself to the rules of the drama?

" Is there any satisfactory evidence of the degeneracy of the *stature* of mankind since the early ages of the world; or of a diminution of stature in particular nations, proportionate to their progress in refinement and luxury?

" Was there less delicacy in the *manners* of the Greeks and Romans, especially towards the female sex, than prevails in modern Europe, and which is generally attributed to the institution of chivalry?

" What combination of circumstances, in an age of ignorance and contention, introduced the refined principles of truth, honour, and decorum, &c. which constituted an essential part of the character of the knights of chivalry?

" To what extent is *artifice* requisite and admissible in works of taste?

" Whether has *science* or *literature* a more powerful influence on the happiness of mankind?

" Does the study of the fine arts, and especially of poetry, tend to the improvement of *practical morality?*

" What are we to understand by the inquiry respecting a *standard* of taste? Can *reason* appeal to a higher power than itself?

" Whether is a temperament of *apathy* or of *great sensibility* most conducive to happiness?

And what combination of the latter with *judgment* is requisite to form a temperament that shall be capable of arriving the nearest to perfect happiness?

" Is *luxury* the principal or sole *cause* of the *vices* of nations? Or are they not the *concomitant effects* of the gradual refinement of the understanding, and the consequent discoveries of means of gratifying the numerous suggestions that imagination, in the progress of its cultivation, excites?

" Is *genius* a gift of nature, or the child of accident; depending upon education, early associations, &c.?

" If genius be a natural power, does the *direction* of it into particular channels, as towards eloquence, music, painting, &c., depend upon nature, or the casual impression of external circumstances?

" Does the theory of a ' moral *sense* ' imply any thing more than a general notion of *benevolence* and *sympathy;* and not an innate power of discerning the *criterion of moral rectitude?*

" Is it true that phosphorescent bodies which

emit *red* light continue to emit this colour to whatever other prismatic rays they be applied? This would seem to prove the mutual convertibility of the different coloured rays.

" Is the luminous appearance of putrescent fish, decayed wood, &c., produced from the actual disengagement of *phosphorated hydrogen gas?* What are the appearances in the various gases? Humboldt says that decayed wood lost its phosphorescence in *azote* and *hydrogen*. But fish shine under water.

" What light might be thrown upon the nature of mineral productions by fusing various proportions of the different earths, and obtaining *crystallites* by slow cooling?

" Do the permanently elastic fluids, in assuming their gaseous form, absorb as much *caloric* as the non-permanent vapours?

" Does the motion of plants depend solely on the state of fulness or depletion in their vessels, on the discharge of an elastic fluid, &c.? How can this be effected by mechanical means? Darkness and moisture, or whatever debilitates, occasion the sleep or collapse of plants.

" Does *oxygen* promote or retard vegetation? Experiments are contradictory on this subject. Oxy-muriatic acid promotes vegetation and germination greatly: the mineral acids, some neutral salts, also. Opium is extremely injurious to plants, but not to the *poppy*. Plants grow better in metallic oxides, as minium and manganese, than in earth.

" Does any absorption or extrication of gas take place through the shell of eggs during incubation? or what is the chick's succedaneum for respiration?

" Do plants, while growing, decompose *water*, or *carbonic acid?* Do they flourish in *hydrogen gas?* or in *carbonic acid gas*, as maintained by Drs. PERCIVAL and HUNTER? Or is *carbonic acid gas* destructive to them, as maintained by PRIESTLEY? What is the nature of the matter which they perspire in different circumstances?

" What is the effect of water, heated to an intense degree in PAPIN's digester, on mineral bodies?

" Upon what part of the composition of the *aluminous* schist does its destructive quality to vegetable life depend ? Upon the *magnesia* which Mr. TENANT has found deleterious to vegetation?

" Can saline, aromatic, and other substances be present in the blood, when we are unable to discover them ? What combinations preserve them from detection? and how does it happen that they again appear in the secretions?

" Does the coagulation of the blood depend upon the contact of *air*, as stated by Mr. HEWSON? or does it coagulate sooner *in vacuo*, as affirmed by Mr. HUNTER?

" To what extent is *imperfect nutrition* from *bad food* to be deemed the great cause of the numerous chronic diseases of the middle ages? viz. scurvy, leprosy, ergot, malum mortuum, &c. ?

" The general neglect of medical literature ; and the consequent repetition of old facts as original discoveries."

To return from this glance at the varied occupations of his mind, always thus directed to some object of usefulness : the affection of his sight began in the summer of 1816; and he always himself attributed it entirely to an attack of head-ache which he had just before suffered from. Yet it is probable that it might rather have been produced by the unremitting use of his eyes, more particularly after he applied them so much to making coloured drawings of diseases of the skin, as they had been weakened, especially that which was now the first and most seriously affected, by repeated inflammation in his childhood. Could he have reconciled himself to retire a few miles into the country, and spend his summer there in entire rest after the severe illness of 1817, it would seem now that there might have been a better hope of his life being prolonged. But an epidemic fever had then begun in LONDON, and his zeal was not to be restrained. He recommenced his attendance at the Fever Institution in the month of April of that year; and from that time to the beginning of the following February he spent from an hour and a half to two hours, or two and a half, daily, in the wards of that hospital, having the care there, in the course of that time, of nearly 700 patients. Such was his anxiety to watch the progress of the epidemic, that nothing could induce him to relax his labours until after all the officers, and most, as it was said, of the attendants of the Institution had suffered from the contagion. He was indeed himself attacked with fever in February, and at first believed it to be the epidemic. But beginning to recover in a very few days, he was disposed then to attribute it more to the fatigue and extreme anxiety he had undergone. These had been at that time much increased by his attendance besides on Dr. DA COSTA, a promising young physician, who, after assisting him a few weeks in the Institution for the sake of becoming acquainted with his practice there, fell a sacrifice to the contagion. From the effects which Dr. BATEMAN experienced from fatigue ever after 1815, it is probable he was right in his conclusion. But however this might be, he never recovered any tolerable degree of strength, but went on rather declining than improving, until in July, 1819, he was taken ill on his road from LONDON to MIDDLETON in DURHAM, whither he was proceeding for the benefit of the sulphureous water of that place, and with difficulty reached BISHOP BUR-

TON, a village near BEVERLEY in YORKSHIRE, the abode of a near relative.

Medical practitioners are often placed in the difficult predicament which involved Dr. BATEMAN after his first protracted and alarming illness, when, while but imperfectly recovered, he resumed his post at the Fever Institution, the duties of which had become of immediate and pressing importance by the rise and spreading of the epidemic, and in the discharge of which he was so indefatigable. They cannot always transfer their cares to satisfactory hands; and, if they could, the strong interest with which they are gradually blended in the mind, and the continual hope that to-morrow will be better with them than to-day, irresistibly persuade them that to quit their post is as unnecessary as it would be dishonourable. On themselves they can hardly be prevailed upon to bestow a thought. It is not that they cling either to fame or emolument. They cling to nothing but their duty; and to that they hold fast until they can hold no longer. There is no reason in this country to complain that the medical profession is inadequately remunerated or honoured. Yet it is probable that few persons out of it are aware of the extent of that zeal and disinterestedness with which medical men of all ranks often persevere in their arduous services to the last. It would not be easy to exhibit a more entire abnegation of self than would be brought to light, if the unboasted, and often gratuitous, ministrations, which are thus ceaselessly going on in secret, could be set before the public eye. But this neither can be, nor ought to be. It is better as it is, for science, for mankind, and for themselves. It may be permitted, nevertheless, to lament over that untimely end, which not very uncommonly is the melancholy consequence of this extreme exclusion of all personal considerations. The great purpose of such devotedness, honourable as it is, is defeated; while by a resolute determination, before it were too late, to forego every view but such as competent judges could approve for the individual concerned, after a careful deliberation upon his circumstances, valuable talents might be preserved for a future and still more important season, perhaps for a long career of usefulness. This would seem to be the only safe way of seeking his decision; to submit with what tranquillity he can to take the place of a patient; and then to resign himself, as he has been accustomed to exact of others, altogether to the advice of those whom he has chosen for his advisers. Thus, doubtless, might not seldom an invaluable life be spared to friends who otherwise, although they see the coming calamity clearer every hour, implore in vain; and to the community who, however little able to estimate the real extent of the loss which they deplore, would easily judge aright of that larger good which might so be reserved. A remarkable instance for the encouragement of practitioners so situated may be found in the history of the late justly eminent Mr. HEY of LEEDS, who, being early in his professional life interrupted by sickness, withdrew from business altogether for several months under very trying circumstances. He returned in health, and with what success and distinction need not be repeated here.

Dr. BATEMAN's health proving at length unequal to such exertions as he had hitherto made, he had resigned his office of Physician to the Fever Institution, after he had discharged it faithfully fourteen years, in the spring of 1818; and was in consequence appointed Consulting Physician. But he endeavoured to serve its cause with what ability he could; and published then an account of the epidemic. And if we regard the soundness of his judgment, the opportunities which he enjoyed, and the talent for accuracy of observation, which he was acknowledged to possess, we must admit that he was peculiarly qualified for the task which he undertook. Whilst the candid and perspicuous statement which he has given of his opinions and his practice render this work truly valuable, he explicitly avows the change which had taken place in his views and methods of treatment; but vindicates medicine from the charge of variable doctrines by referring in his preface to the alteration in the characters of disease, as explaining what might otherwise be attributed to fashion and novelty.

In discussing the very considerable change not only in the treatment of Fever, but likewise in the symptoms by which the disease is characterised, he offers an ingenious explanation of the difference in the supposition that formerly by the exclusion of fresh air, and by the excess of the stimulating plan, the powers of the system must have been exhausted; and that the ensuing symptoms of debility, which were regarded as the essential feature of the malady, might be merely an effect resulting from the injudicious measures adopted.

Dr. BATEMAN next collected his REPORTS on the Diseases of LONDON from the EDINBURGH MEDICAL AND SURGICAL JOURNAL into a volume, to which he prefixed an interesting and able historical sketch of the state of health in LONDON at different periods during the last century, containing an investigation of the causes which might be supposed to have led to its improved condition.

This sketch or survey he had published originally in a periodical work he was connected with, which did not proceed.

But although now, being relieved from the most urgent of his public duties, he could devote more attention to his own health, and more time to relaxation, his benefit from this change in his circumstances was inconsiderable. He could hardly be said to recover strength, or to be in any way much better.

In the summer of 1819, as has been already mentioned, he left LONDON therefore for YORKSHIRE; and the farther attack of illness which he suffered there, determined him finally to forego all thought of returning to practice in the metropolis; and he consequently resigned his appointment at the Public Dispensary. His long and assiduous services to that very valuable charity were acknowledged on this occasion by a vote for a piece of plate to be presented to him, and his nomination as a Life Governor, as in the cases of his respected friends and predecessors, Dr. WILLAN and Mr. PEARSON. But he declined to accede to a proposal of naming him Consulting Physician, on the ground of his having now retired to so great a distance from LONDON. With this reply he stated also his intention of resigning the appointment which he still held of Consulting Physician to the Fever Institution. It would have gratified him the more to accept the proposal here adverted to but for his objection to an honour which implied a trust he had no longer the means of discharging; because it originated with his excellent friend and colleague at the Dispensary, Doctor LAIRD; for whom he retained through life an affectionate respect and regard. They had been fellow-students at EDINBURGH, and had entered upon the practice of their profession together in LONDON. The community of their interests and occupations had, from the beginning of their acquaintance, favoured that familiar intimacy which Dr. BATEMAN so much enjoyed with men who were labouring in the fields of knowledge with similar tastes and views to his own. " For twenty years," says Dr. LAIRD, " we were acquainted and engaged in similar professional pursuits and duties. Shall the lapse of a few months efface the impressions of years? Can we cease to deplore the premature interruption of that intercourse which was at once so instructive and so pleasing, or to dwell with grateful remembrance on the virtues we loved, and the talents we admired?"

Such friendships (and this was one which Dr. BATEMAN peculiarly valued, for it was uninterrupted and still growing through all those years,) very happily connect that delightful period of professional life which is spent in the schools with its subsequent course through the difficulties and vicissitudes of practice. It is not always that they are so judiciously formed, or that future circumstances coincide so agreeably with their promotion. But when they are thus fortunate, the pleasures they provide are not seldom accompanied with the substantial advantage of such reciprocal advice and assistance in many of the more ordinary matters of business, as well as in greater emergencies, as no other sources can supply. And with a view to this comfort it is to be wished that the warmth with which young men, suddenly brought together for the same important objects, and unused before to equal gratifications in society, could be so far guarded that they might not rush at once into connections difficult to be got clear of, and of irretrievable injury to their present business, and therefore to their future success. With a very little patience they will see, whether they look for them or not, what are the characters, and what the dispositions, of those who surround them; and they will be far safer in leaving an association of so much moment to their credit as well as their good, to that instinctive attraction which never fails in due season to bring together those of a congenial turn, to separate the chaff from the wheat, than in any hasty choice upon the first impulses of their own sanguine inexperience.

The alarming languors in which Dr. BATEMAN was thought to be dying by all around him as well as by himself, and to which he had first become subject during his severe illness in 1817, returned upon him continually at the period at which this narrative has now arrived, especially after using the least bodily exertion, so that it proved to be impossible to attempt to return with him to WHITBY as had been intended. He was removed therefore to a temporary habitation at BISHOP BURTON, for the sake of the greater quiet which he might enjoy there than in the large family of his sister.

During the ensuing winter of 1819—1820, he gradually improved in strength there, so as to be able to take gentle exercise on a pony, or in a gig, almost daily; but on the return of warm weather, early in April, he had a severe attack of languor, after a short ride. His dread of these attacks was so great, and they returned so frequently after the smallest fatigue, that he gradually relinquished all exertion, as he even apprehended the effort of walking across the room might prove fatal, having for some time, it was supposed, suspected some organic affection of the heart, and become more fearful, on that account, of the consequences of exertion. Thus the improvement in his health which seemed to have taken place after his recovery from the effects of the severe attack of illness, (or return, as it might be considered, of his former ailment,) which had seized him on his journey into the country in the July before adverted to, proved to be transitory, and he ultimately became the subject of a progressive affection of the digestive organs, accompanied with great exhaustion of strength, but without fever, or any manifest structural disease, of the fatal tendency of which he had himself the strongest impression.

He passed the whole of Sunday, the 9th of April, in a state of extraordinary suffering from languor, and a variety of nervous feelings which he always said it was impossible to describe, farther than that they were inconceivably painful and distressing. He went to bed at night with a firm persuasion on his own mind that he should never again rise from it: and in fact he did confine himself to it for the following three weeks from the mere apprehension of the effects of exertion.

And now we are come to a period of his life, and to circumstances respecting which it was natural that many difficulties should be felt in regard to a public biographical memoir, the circulation of which was to be looked for chiefly in the scientific world. For although the reputation of Dr. BATEMAN was such as to create a just expectation of some such account, the habit of modern times discouraged much detail of matters not supposed to be directly connected with that exclusive aspect which belonged to his public character. Yet, without entering here into any question of the fidelity or the wisdom of that habit as a general practice, how could there be any satisfaction in giving forth as a life what omitted a very material and important portion of its facts! The proper duty of the biographer in such a case appeared to be, to prepare a faithful narrative of all that was known concerning the subject of it, so as to leave out no part of the truth, and to commit it, thus entire, to the public judgment.

In the mean time, and before any conclusion had been settled, the substance of those passages in Dr. BATEMAN's life now alluded to was committed to paper at a particular request; and, being thought worthy of preservation by the very respectable clergyman to whom it had been communicated, was by him, without any such benefit from his own hand as its author had hoped for, immediately sent to the press. From the CHRISTIAN OBSERVER it was soon unexpectedly republished by another party, with the same view to usefulness, in a separate form; and so passed altogether out of its original keeping. To that account, as it so appeared, for it comprised all the facts of importance, nothing can be added. Nor can it be right to subtract from it. It is a plain history of the latter days of a valuable life, as these sheets have so far been of what went before. The object of the whole is to save in one narrative, while it may yet be done, whatever belonged to that life, down to its close.

In the conviction that it would be dishonest to suppress any circumstances material to that end; and in the full persuasion that Dr. BATEMAN would not himself have been deterred from the publication by any apprehension of the manner in which it might be received, but would, on the contrary, have been anxious for it, in the hope of benefiting others, what remains to be told is therefore here repeated from the manuscript just mentioned.

" In the midst of the zeal and industry with which Dr. BATEMAN had continued his pursuit of science and literature, he had contrived," says the eye-witness of the days we have thus reached, " to mix with his severer studies, so long as his health permitted, a large portion of the dissipations of gay society. And he carried with him into both these opposite pursuits an energy of mind and of feeling which rendered him more than ordinarily susceptible of the enjoyments which either of them can afford. He always retained a high 'sense of honour,' as it is called, and was strictly careful to avoid, in all his conduct, every thing that the world esteems discreditable. He lived, however, to see and to feel, what at that time he had no conception of, — how meagre a system of morality is that which the world is satisfied with, compared with the comprehensive morality of the Gospel — that Christian 'holiness' without which 'no man shall see the Lord.' His habits of life thus concurring with the natural corruption of the human heart, and estranging him more and more from God, he soon became confirmed in his leaning to the doctrine of Materialism, which he had been already tempted to adopt during the pursuit of his anatomical and physiological studies at EDINBURGH. This lamentable tendency was strongly increased by the society which he now fell into of some men of considerable talent, who had already espoused all the principles of that unhappy system; and though never able *fully* to embrace those opinions himself, he was yet sufficiently influenced by them to become sceptical respecting the truth of Divine Revelation, and was, therefore, of course, a stranger to the hopes, as well as negligent of the duties, of Christianity.

" In the summer of 1815 his health began to decline, and in the following year a complaint in his eyes came on, which threatened loss of sight, and precluded him from all his accustomed sources of occupation and amusement. Under these circumstances it was that I became his constant companion and attendant; and for four years had the misery of witnessing his total estrangement from God and religion.

" It was on Sunday, the 9th of April (the day lately noticed), that he first spoke to me on the subject of religion.

"Religion was a subject which, for many reasons, had never been discussed between us. Though the tenor of his life had made me but too well acquainted with the state of his mind, he had always avoided any declaration of his opinions, knowing the pain it would give me to hear them. He was habitually fond of argument, and skilled in it; and I knew that I was quite incompetent to argue with him. I considered, too, that the habit of disputing in favour of any opinion only serves, in general, to rivet it more firmly in the mind; men commonly finding their own arguments more convincing than those of their adversaries. And, above all, I knew that this was a case in which mere argument must always be insufficient, — for 'it is with the heart that man believeth unto righteousness;' and in most, if not all cases of scepticism, the will and the affections need to be set right even more than the understanding; and upon these, *argument* can have no influence. On the evening of the day I have mentioned, Dr. BATEMAN had been expressing to me his conviction that he could not live much longer, and complaining of the dreadful nervous sensations which continually harassed him; and then he added, 'but all these sufferings are a just punishment for my long scepticism, and neglect of God and religion.' This led to a conversation, in the course of which he observed that medical men were very generally sceptical, and that the mischief arose from what he considered a natural tendency of some of their studies to lead to materialism. I replied, that the mischief appeared to me to originate rather in their neglect to examine into the evidences of the truth of the Bible, *as an actual revelation from God;* because, if a firm conviction of that were once established, the authority of the Scriptures must be paramount, and the tendency of all inferior studies, in opposition to their declarations, could have no weight. He said, he believed I was right, and that he had, in fact, been intending to examine fully into the subject, when the complaint in his eyes came on and shut him out from reading. Our conversation ended in his permitting me to read to him the first of SCOTT's 'Essays on some of the most Important Subjects in Religion,' which treats of ' The Divine Inspiration of the Scriptures.' He listened with intense earnestness, and, when it was concluded, exclaimed, ' This is demonstration! complete demonstration!' He then asked me to read to him the account given in the New Testament of the resurrection of our Saviour: which I did from all the four evangelists. I read also many other passages of Scripture, with some of which he was extremely struck; especially with that declaration, that ' the natural man receiveth not the things of the spirit of God, for they are foolishness unto him: neither can he know them, because they are spiritually discerned.'

"For two or three days he showed increasing interest in the subject of religion; and I read to him continually the Scriptures, and other books which seemed to me best calculated to give him the information he thirsted for. When I went into his room a few mornings after, he said, ' It is quite impossible to describe to you the change which has taken place in my mind; I feel as if a new world was opened to me, and all the interests and pursuits of *this* have faded into nothing in comparison with it. They seem so mean, and paltry, and insignificant, that my blindness in living so long immersed in them, and devoted to them, is quite inconceivable and astonishing to myself.' He often expressed, in the strongest terms, and with many tears, his deep repentance, and his abhorrence of himself for his former sinful life and rebellion against God; but he seemed to have from the first so clear a view of the all-sufficiency of the Saviour's atonement, and of the Christian scheme of salvation, as freed him at once from that distrust of forgiveness which is so apt to afflict persons on the first sight of their sins, and of the purity and holiness of Him ' with whom they have to do.' The self-abasing views which he entertained of himself necessarily enhanced his sense of the pardoning love and mercy of God in Christ Jesus, thus graciously extended to him; and which he felt so strongly, that he was filled with the liveliest emotions of gratitude and joy, and in this happy state continued for several days.

" He soon, however, experienced an afflicting reverse of feeling. One evening I left him to visit a near relative, at that time confined to her room in a precarious state of health; and his mother, who had been in attendance upon her, took my place at the bedside of her son. Dr. BATEMAN told her that I had been reading to him various detached portions of Scripture, and that he now wished to hear the New Testament read regularly through from the beginning. She consequently began to read, and had proceeded as far as the tenth chapter of St. MATTHEW, when he suddenly exclaimed, that he could not believe in the miracles of the Saviour, and that therefore he must perish for ever. It needs scarcely be pointed out how much more properly this might be called *temptation* to unbelief, than *unbelief* itself. While the difficulty of believing was felt, the awful consequences of not believing were fully admitted, that is, were firmly *believed.* This suggestion of his spiritual enemy threw him into a state of the most dreadful anguish, and I was immediately sent for to his bedside. On my arrival he had become a little more composed, but was still in great agitation, and was praying in agony 'to be saved, and not to be given up to this dreadful state of unbelief.' To comfort his mind, we said what we could from Scripture, and from the experience of other Christians; and he was a little relieved by hearing some passages from an Essay in the volume before mentioned, 'On the Warfare and Experience of Believers;' finding that his was not, as he had supposed, a case of new occurrence; but that the author of that work was already acquainted with its symptoms, and augured favourably of them as often accompanying the progress of religion in the soul. Still the idea that his death was fast approaching, and that there was no hope of his mind being convinced before it arrived, quite overwhelmed him. Feeling ourselves to be very inadequate guides and comforters in these afflicting circumstances, we gladly adopted the suggestion of a friend that we should request a neighbouring clergyman, of piety and judgment, to visit him. Dr. BATEMAN himself grasped eagerly at the proposal, and I wrote immediately to the clergyman in question; but he was from home, and was not expected to return for two or three weeks. A few days after this unwelcome intelligence, Dr. BATEMAN told me he had no doubt this disappointment was for his good; and that it was better for him to be left to himself, as he did not think any thing could have convinced him so fully of *the efficacy of prayer*, as the sensible relief which he experienced from it during those conflicts of doubt and unbelief with which his mind continued to be harassed. He added, that he now spent whole nights in prayer. He felt perfectly assured that his doubts were the suggestions of the great adversary of souls; and remarked, that they were vividly and manifestly darted, as it were, into his mind, instead of arising from his own reflections, or resulting from any train of reasoning; and the absurdity of them, in many instances, was so obvious, that his judgment detected it at once, though he still had not power to drive them from the hold they took of his imagination, or to banish them, for the time, from his thoughts. These paroxysms of distress and conflict, which sometimes lasted many hours, he continued subject to for about a fortnight; but they gradually became less long and violent, and he experienced increasing relief from prayer during their continuance, till at length they subsided entirely, and left his mind satisfied on all those points which had before presented so many obstacles to his belief.

"About this time he received an unexpected visit from a medical friend, who, with great difficulty, succeeded in persuading him that he was by no means in that state of danger and debility which he had apprehended, and that he had the *power* of taking exercise if he could but exert sufficient resolution to attempt it. Experiment convinced him that this opinion was correct: he was prevailed upon to leave his bed, and in a very few days was able to be some hours daily in the open air, and to take considerable exercise; and it is remarkable that from this time he had no return of languor after fatigue, except in one instance. Thus was he delivered, by the gracious Providence of God, from those overwhelming apprehensions of immediate death which had been so instrumental in bringing him to CHRIST, as soon as they had effected that blessed purpose.

" He now rarely spoke of the state of his mind and feelings; for such was the extreme reserve of his character, that it could only be overcome by deep and powerful emotions.; and when no longer agitated by these, he returned to his natural habits, and was silent on the subject that most deeply interested him. Still it was abundantly evident that it *did* interest him. The avidity with which he listened to the word of God — his eagerness to attend public worship (which for many years he had entirely neglected), and the heartfelt and devout interest which he obviously took in the service — his enlarged and active benevolence — the change which had taken place in his tastes, inclinations, and pursuits — all testified that he was indeed ' brought out of darkness into marvellous light;' ' old things had passed away, and all things had become new.'

" In the course of the summer his health and strength were considerably recruited; but towards the close of it a little over exertion in walking brought on an accession of fever, and a great aggravation of all the symptoms of his disorder; but still he continued able to take a little exercise. While he remained in the country he had much leisure, which was devoted entirely to religious reading: for every other subject had now become insipid and uninteresting to him; and never did the pursuits of science and literature afford him such vivid enjoyment as he now received from these hallowed studies. In November he removed to WHITBY for the winter; and his health continued in much the same state till a short time before Christmas, when a walk rather longer than usual again produced increased fever and debility, and from that period his strength and appetite visibly declined, while his spirit was as visibly ripening for heaven: his faith and patience were strengthened; his hope increased, his charity enlarged; yet he was naturally so extremely reserved in the expression of his feelings, that he rarely spoke of them till within the last month of his life, when he rejoiced ' with a joy unspeakable and full of glory,' which bore down all opposition; for he experienced a happiness to which all the accumulated enjoyments of his whole previous life could bear no proportion or comparison, even that 'peace of God' which 'passeth all understanding,' and which must be felt, or at least witnessed, in order to form any just conception of its nature and effects. What a striking example did he now exhibit to us! From his early youth he had devoted himself with delight and industry to the acquisition of knowledge, and the pursuits of literature and science; and he had *'had his reward'* in the honour and reputation which success had procured for him, —a reward which he keenly enjoyed and very highly prized. Those who have known *only* the pleasures which arise from worldly gratifications surely ought to recollect, that, being confessedly ignorant of those spiritual enjoyments which they despise, they cannot be competent to decide upon their reality or their value; it belongs only to those who have experienced *both*, to appreciate either. And how did Dr. BATEMAN appreciate them? In contrasting, as he frequently did, his present happiness with all that he had formerly enjoyed and *called* happiness, he seemed always at a loss to find words to express how poor, and mean, and despicable all earthly gratifications appeared to him, when compared with that 'joy and peace in believing,' which now filled his soul: and, 'one particle of which,' he sometimes said, 'ten thousand worlds would not tempt him to part with.' And it should be remembered that this was not the evidence of a man disappointed in his worldly pursuits: he had already, as before observed, 'had his reward' in this world — he had experienced the utmost success in the path which he had chosen — he had been keenly susceptible of intellectual pleasures; and of these, as well as of all inferior amusements, he had enjoyed more than a common portion; but when the only object that can satisfy the affections and fill the capacities of a rational and immortal being was revealed to him — when he viewed by the eye of faith that 'life and immortality' which are 'brought to light' by the Gospel — earthly fame, and honour, and pleasure, sank into the dust; and, in reflecting upon his past life, the only thing that gave him any satisfaction was the hope that his labours might have been beneficial to his fellow-creatures, for whom his charity had now become unbounded. He often said that 'the blessing of his conversion was never out of his mind day or night; that it was a theme of perpetual thanksgiving; and that he never awoke in the night without being overwhelmed with joy and gratitude in the recollection of it.' He always spoke of his long bodily afflictions with the most devout thankfulness, as having been instrumental in bringing him to God; and considered his almost total blindness as an especial mercy, because, by shutting out external objects, it had enabled him to devote his mind more entirely to spiritual things. Often, latterly, he expressed an ardent desire to 'depart and to be with Christ;' but always added, that he was cheerfully willing to wait the Lord's pleasure, certain that if he was continued in this world it was only for his own good, and to make him more 'meet to be a partaker of the inheritance of the saints in light.'

"He bore his bodily afflictions with the most

exemplary patience, and even cheerfulness, and continually expressed his thankfulness that they were not greater; sometimes saying, 'What a blessing it is to be allowed to slip gently and gradually out of life as I am doing!' He would not allow any one to speak of his *sufferings*, always saying, 'they did not deserve a stronger name than inconveniences.' He neither complained himself, nor would permit others to complain for him. Once, when the nurse who attended him said, 'Oh that cough! how troublesome it is!' he replied, 'Have a little patience, nurse; I shall soon be in a better world; and what a glorious change that will be!' Indeed, the joy of his mind seemed to have absorbed all sense of his physical sufferings. I once remarked to him, that he appeared to have experienced no intermission of these joyful feelings; and he answered, 'For some months past *never*, and never the smallest rising of any thing like impatience or complaint.' His mind, naturally active and ardent, retained all its powers in full vigour to the last moment of his life, and was never once clouded or debilitated even in the most depressing nervous languors. Indeed, after the whole current of his tastes and affections had been turned into a new channel, its ardour and activity rather increased than diminished, from the deep conviction which he felt of the superiority of his present views and pursuits to all that had hitherto engrossed him. During the last week of his life, especially, the strength and clearness of his intellect and of his spiritual perceptions, were very remarkable; and on its being one day observed to him, that as his bodily powers decayed, those of his soul seemed to become more vigorous, he replied, 'They do, exactly in an inverse ratio : I have been very sensible of it.'

"He conversed with the greatest animation all the day, and almost all the night, preceding his death, principally on the joys of heaven, and the glorious change he was soon to experience; often exclaiming, 'What a happy hour will the hour of death be !' He dwelt much on the description of the NEW JERUSALEM in the Revelation of St. JOHN, and listened with great delight to several passages from BAXTER's 'Saint's

Rest,' and some of WATTS's Hymns on the same subject. Once in the night he said to his mother, ' Surely you are not in tears! Mine is a case that calls for rejoicing, and not for sorrow. Only think what it will be to drop this poor, frail, perishing body, and go to the glories that are set before me!' Not more than an hour before his death, when he had been expressing his faith and hope in very animated terms, I remarked to him how striking the uniformity of faith and of feeling expressed by believers in the same circumstance, at every distance of time and place, and spoke of it as an indisputable evidence that these graces are wrought in all by 'one and the self-same spirit,' and as a proof of the truth of the Bible, the promises and descriptions of which are thus so strikingly fulfilled and exemplified. He entered into the argument with his accustomed energy, and assented to its truth with delight. It seemed remarkable, that though he had during his whole illness been very sensible of his increasing weakness, and had watched and marked accurately all its gradations, yet he spoke, in the last moments of his life, of going down stairs as usual (he had been carried up and down for several days), and said 'it could not require more than a very few weeks now to wear him out;' not appearing to be at all aware that his end was so very near, till about half an hour before his death. Finding himself extremely languid, he took a little milk, and desired that air might be admitted into the room; and on being asked if he felt relieved at all, said, 'Very little: I can hardly distinguish, indeed, whether this is languor or drowsiness which has come over me; but it is a very *agreeable* feeling.' Soon after, he said suddenly, 'I surely must be going now, my strength sinks so fast, I have almost lost the power of moving my limbs;' and on my making some observation on the glorious prospect before him, he added, 'Oh, yes! I am GLAD to go, if it be the LORD's will!' He shut his eyes, and lay quite composed, and by and by said, 'What glory! the angels are waiting for me!' — then, after another short interval of quiet, added, 'Lord JESUS, receive my soul!' and to those who were about him, 'Farewell!'

These were the last words he spoke: he gradually and gently sunk away, and in about ten minutes breathed his last, calmly and without a struggle, at nine in the morning of the 9th of April, the very day on which, twelve months before, his mind had first been awakened to the hopes and joys of the ever-blessed Gospel!

"What a contrast did his actual departure form with what I had reason to apprehend, when I watched over his couch in LONDON, expecting that every moment would be his last; and when, with a hard indifference and insensibility, he talked only of going to his 'last sleep!' And how can I worthily acknowledge the goodness of Almighty God, who effected such a change in his state?

"It appears that he preceded his revered, though unknown, instructor, Mr. SCOTT, exactly one week. He never ceased to remember, with the deepest gratitude, his obligations to that excellent man. It was only the evening before his death that he was recommending, with great fervency, to a young friend, whose mother, under affliction, was first beginning to enquire after religious truth, to engage her to read 'SCOTT's Essays,' acknowledging with fervent gratitude the benefit he had himself received from that work, and concluding an animated eulogium by saying, 'How have I prayed for that man!' What a blessed meeting may we not suppose they have had in the world of glory.

"The medical friend before alluded to has remarked, that 'the entire simplicity and sincerity of Dr. BATEMAN's natural character give additional value to all that fell from him. He never used a language that was *at all* at variance with his real feelings, and was in no degree given to vain imaginations.' This testimony is very true, and this remarkable simplicity and sobriety of his natural character remained unaltered in the great revolution which took place in his principles and dispositions; he went into no exaggerations of feeling, or excesses of enthusiasm. And surely the merciful Providence which preserved his sound understanding in all its integrity, to the last moment of his life, must silence the gainsayer and the 'disputer of this world,' who might strive to attribute the sacred influence of religion on his mind to the errors of an intellect impaired by long disease and suffering."

With the preceding paragraph the narrative, which was published in the manner already explained, concluded. Some objections, which were suggested to the friends of Dr. BATEMAN, against the propriety of detailing his scepticism and subsequent conversion in a memoir of his life, proposed to be published in a periodical medical work, drew forth the following reply. The appearance of this correspondence in print was indeed altogether unexpected by the parties concerned in it; but as it has been so many times appended to the successive editions of the Memoir, the answer to those objections is here inserted for the sake of its connection with the principles which in the first instance dictated the manuscript record.

" With respect to the mention of Dr. BATEMAN's conversion, and of his previous unbelief, we are not, it seems, agreed. It appears to me that biography, like history, to answer its best and most valuable purposes, should be a faithful narrative of *facts* ; so that, even setting aside the general obligation to truth and fidelity, I should, if I were writing a memoir, think it as necessary not to suppress defects and faults, as not to create or exaggerate virtues. That Dr. BATEMAN's character for morality would stand high in the world, I make no doubt; for he never lost the influence of his early education and habits, and was always careful to avoid in all his conduct every thing that the world calls discreditable. Yet it was from the defectiveness of his moral views and principles, which on many occasions was manifest to my observation, as well as from his neglect of all religious duties, that I was led to infer with certainty that his religious belief was wrong, though I never heard him express a single sceptical sentiment: and his conversion would have given me little satisfaction, if it had produced no change but in the state of his *feelings:* we have a more severe and safer test, — ' by their *fruits* ye shall know them.' The change which took place in his conduct and dispositions was quite as obvious as that which affected his feelings and views; he evidenced the soundness of his conversion by realising the description of the Apostle: he was 'a new creature;' 'old things had passed away, and *all things*,' principles, motives, tastes, affections, dispositions, conduct, '*all things* had become new'—vices which before he had tolerated, he now abhorred: his acquisition of humility, that truly Christian virtue, was especially striking; and the almost total eradication of selfishness, with the substitution of the most enlarged benevolence, generosity, and kindness, was little less so: opportunities of doing good to the bodies and souls of men were not only *not omitted*, they were sought out and improved with zealous activity, and it was gratifying to see with what constant cheerfulness and readiness his own ease and pleasure and convenience were relinquished, whenever they interfered with the wants of the meanest of his fellow-creatures. No, my dear friend, we need not leave it to the unbeliever to say that 'to him religion was not necessary;' 'men do not gather grapes of thorns, or figs of thistles:' no merely human motives, no motives,

I mean, which have their origin and their end in this life, ever produced such a character and such a conduct as he now exhibited. The morality of the world differs from that of the Christian, as the counterfeit differs from the jewel, and this difference was never more strikingly displayed than in Dr. BATEMAN, before and after his conversion. That his mind became more susceptible of the impressions of religion through the influence of suffering and affliction, is a fact which I should not seek to hide, and upon which no objection could, I think, be justly founded; it is in itself, on the contrary, a confirmation of many of the declarations of Scripture; and it is matter of common observation and experience, that while man *retains the power* to enjoy and to pursue earthly things, he rarely looks for higher sources of gratification; but when affliction or disappointment, or some striking providence, has opened his eyes to the delusions of the world, and shown him its utter insufficiency to provide him with any substantial happiness, then only two alternatives remain for him; either with our blessed friend, he 'acquaints himself with GOD and *is at peace*,' and exclaims with him, and with David, and with thousands of the servants of God in all ages, 'It is good for me that I have been afflicted!' or else he drags on a listless and insipid existence, without interest and without enjoyment, which too often ends in open profaneness and immorality. That religion, then, can afford to man consolation and joy and hope and peace, when all other resources have failed him, and every earthly gratification has dissolved from his grasp, is a fact that surely cannot be calculated to bring discredit upon it.

"It was not the fault of Dr. BATEMAN's *judgment* that he so long remained in ignorance of those important truths which afterward brought such powerful conviction to his mind, for he had long seen the necessity of enquiring into their evidences, and determined at some time or other to enter upon it, when he was shut out from reading by the affection of his sight; the cause was to be found rather in the *perversion of his affections*, which were devoted to earthly things; and it requires but little observation on ourselves and others to convince us how little, in general, *judgment* influences the conduct, if it be powerfully opposed by inclination: he did not *find* the blessings of religion till he *sought* them. '*Ask* and it shall be given you — *seek* and ye shall find,'—the promise is explicit and positive, the condition is natural and reasonable: and it is no inconsiderable evidence to the truth of Scripture that its promises are thus fulfilled, and its descriptions realised, in the daily experience of individuals throughout all ages and generations of men. Neither should I hesitate for fear of objections which might be drawn from the morbid state of his nervous sensations at the time when the first religious impressions were made upon his mind; he was nervous *then*, no doubt; but he was not at all nervous when, through the remaining year of his life, he devoted all the powers of his vigorous mind and discriminating judgment to the investigation of religion; pursuing it as he would have done any other science, with minute and cautious examination, though with all his characteristic ardour; and that ardour too increased, not so much by the novelty of the pursuit (for I have never been acquainted with a mind so little liable as his was to be affected by *mere* novelty), as by the conviction which was impressed upon him more and more forcibly at every step, as light and knowledge increased, of the infinite value and importance of the subject. I do not see that any solid objection could be founded on the *previous* nervousness, unless it could be proved that the powers of his mind had been weakened by it; and that this was not the case, all who conversed and all who corresponded with him could bear ample testimony. With regard to his profession, he never practised it with more acuteness and zeal, and certainly never with more success, than during the last winter; besides many patients among his old friends and acquaintance in his native place, the poor came to him daily, and he often examined into a case with all his accustomed vigour and discrimination, when he was obliged to dictate a prescription, unable from bodily weakness to use a pen. Still, however, I do not doubt that many people, unwilling to admit the necessary inferences from these facts, would attempt to invalidate the facts themselves, by making the animadversions which have been anticipated. Men are, in general, disposed to ascribe all such remarkable changes as that which we are considering, to some weakness of mind or unsoundness of intellect, to call it, in short, ' foolishness.' Experiment is allowed to be the only basis of sound knowledge in all other sciences, in religion alone it is despised and ridiculed, and we are disbelieved though we only ' speak that we do know, and testify that which we have seen,' and here, therefore, the world and the Christian voluntarily separate :—

" ' She scorns his pleasures, for she knows them not ;
He seeks not hers, for he has proved them vain !' "

To the communication of some other difficulties about the same time followed the answer which will next be copied.

" I cannot but attempt to answer, to the best of my power, the questions you have proposed respecting the process by which Dr. BATEMAN's mind was brought at length to a firm and settled faith. It appears to me that his disbelief of the miracles was a matter of *feeling* rather than of *reasoning*, because it did not spring from his own reflection; it was not a deduction from a chain of argument, but was shot suddenly into his mind upon hearing the narrative of the Redeemer's life as related by the Evangelist: probably it arose in part from the previous habits of his mind. All unbelievers are at times, I suppose, disturbed by fears that they may be mistaken; and though these fears are seldom strong enough to impel them to a full examination of the grounds on which they stand, they are yet sufficient to make them glad to catch at any plausible difficulty which may strengthen them in their scepticism, and, if possible, keep them easy: the miracles present such a difficulty; and hence Dr. BATEMAN had been accustomed to rest upon it; and it was therefore not surprising that when the subject was presented to his mind for the *first time* after he had become a believer, his old objections should have recurred, and his new and weak faith, for which he had not yet learned to 'give a reason,' have been unsettled by them. As his disbelief had not been occasioned, so neither was it removed, by reasoning. The only argument which I remember to have urged to him on the subject was this — ' that the *omniscience* of the Saviour, — that perfect knowledge, not only of the external circumstances, but of all that was passing in the inmost heart of man, which he displayed in his conversations with the Pharisees and the multitude, as well as with his disciples, *was sufficient to prove his Deity;* that St. John not only asserts positively the same truth, but declares also, that ' he made all things, and without him was not any thing made that was made,' and that no one, therefore, who admits these proofs of the Deity of Christ, as Dr. BATEMAN then did, could, with any consistency, doubt his controul over ' the works of his own hands,' his power to still the winds and the sea, or to raise a dead person to life, with a word.' He acknowledged at once the truth of this argument, yet his doubts did not at all give way to it; an inconsistency which seems sufficient of itself to prove that his disbelief was a matter of feeling, independent of reason. There were seasons when his mind was quite free from it; it came in paroxysms; and while these lasted he used to say, that it would hardly be possible to count the ridiculous doubts which thronged into his mind. The absurdity of these doubts was so obvious in many instances, that his mind detected it at once; yet their palpable fallacy and folly did not lessen their impression on his imagination; he had no power to banish them from his thoughts; and what most of all distressed him at these times, was his utter inability to bring his mind to bear upon the subject; he felt as if he could neither think nor argue upon it; his understanding was powerless and passive; and thus he was obliged to submit to that torrent of unbelief and doubt which was poured rapidly through his mind. Prayer, fervent and persevering prayer, is the great 'weapon of our warfare,' the appointed means of communication between God and the soul, and through prayer his deliverance from these harassing conflicts was at length gradually accomplished. If the Lord sometimes ' *waits to be gracious,*' it is only because he sees it to be for our good; let us still go on in the use of the means which he has appointed, remembering his gracious admonition and promise: ' Oh tarry thou the Lord's leisure!' — be ' strong' in patience and perseverance, and assuredly in the end ' he shall comfort thine heart.' Scarcely does he give us one command without annexing some promise to encourage us to obey it. Frequently, no doubt, ' we ask and have not,' but it is ' because we ask amiss.' We pray eagerly for the gratification of our own desires, instead of praying in entire submission to the divine will; we forget that all our prayers should be offered in the spirit of that prayer which our Lord himself has taught us: for it was no doubt the spirit rather than the form, which he meant to inculcate; — ' Thy will be done:' — ' lead us not into temptation, but deliver us from evil.' God alone knows what *is* evil for us; he alone can see where our danger lies and what are our wants, and provide for us the proper guards and remedies. St. Paul himself seems to have fallen into this error, to which we are all liable: he prayed repeatedly and positively, that 'the thorn in the flesh,' from which he seems to have suffered so acutely, might be removed; he knew not the merciful and wise reasons for which it had been sent; he knew not that it was 'lest he should be exalted above measure through the abundance of the revelations' vouchsafed to him, the eminence by which he was distinguished above even the other Apostles; lest, lost in pride and self-conceit, he should, 'after preaching to others, himself have been a cast-away.' Let us not, then, too earnestly desire the removal of doubts and fears, or of any of those trials of our faith and patience with which it is, no doubt, necessary that we should be exercised; we are in the hands of a wise and tender Parent, whose 'grace' is still 'sufficient' for us, whose language to us in all the dispensations of his providence and his grace is, 'What I do, thou knowest not now, but thou shalt know hereafter,' and who has promised to 'make all things work together for good' to them that love him.' Only let us remember *that we must not be want-*

ing to ourselves; let us ask with the disciples, 'Lord increase our faith!' For 'without faith it is impossible to please God;' and we are expressly told, that it is 'not of ourselves, but is the gift of God;' and that it is also all that is necessary for our salvation. — 'Believe in the Lord Jesus Christ, and thou shalt be saved.' But the pride of man's corrupt heart revolts from the simplicity of dependence upon God in Christ, and he would fain, like Naaman, 'do some great thing' to have part in the merit of his own salvation.

"Do you not think that we are in general prone to depend too much upon human authorities in matters of religion? Men, at the very best, are fallible and imperfect — scarcely two of them are to be found who think alike; all have a considerable alloy of error and infirmity, which must, more or less, tinge and discolour the truth as it passes through their minds; and the greater variety of them we consult, the more likely we are to be perplexed and unsettled by their clashing and divided opinions: surely it is better to go to the word of God itself, and to study it incessantly with fervent prayer, that he will enable us to understand, to feel, and to apply it. What an inexhaustible treasure of divine instruction is supplied to us in the Psalms of David! His experience is minutely detailed, and he is in all things an example of 'a man after God's own heart;' his deep repentance and humiliation, — his abhorrence of sin, because of its offensiveness in the sight of a pure and holy God, — his rapturous love, and gratitude, and adoration, — his firm adherence to God in the midst of that contempt and scorn which a serious profession of religion always provokes from the world, ('The proud have had me exceedingly in derision, yet have I not shrinked from thy law,') — his faith and devotedness — how brightly and powerfully are these and other Christian graces exemplified in his character! Yet, for our comfort and encouragement, we see that they consisted with doubts and unbelief in trying seasons; with, at times, much deadness and coldness of heart and affections: and here again he affords a striking example for our imitation; for in all the vicissitudes of his spiritual life his constant and only resource is PRAYER.

"Dr. BATEMAN's speedy deliverance from his doubts and fears seems to have surprised you; we all differ from each other in the features of our character, and our dispensations of grace are as various, because God, with infinite wisdom and tenderness, adjusts and proportions the one to the other; no man's experience, therefore, can be a rule for another; though the great outlines must be uniform, the detail and the circumstances are infinitely varied; besides, Dr. BATEMAN's time was short;—and as in the natural world, God in his providence has ordered, that where the summer is short, there vegetation shall be rapid; so here, in the kingdom of his grace, ' the Sun of righteousness' having but a little while to shine, the seeds shot rapidly, and the fruits ripened fast.

" I have no doubt that you have accounted justly for the effect produced on Dr. BATEMAN's mind by the perusal of Mr. SCOTT's Essay. ' The preparation of the heart is from the Lord.' All the appointments of Providence and of grace are but so many links in that chain which is to connect the soul with God: thus Dr. BATEMAN was withdrawn from the turmoil and bustle of the world, in which he had been so long immersed, and placed in retirement and quiet; — the society of unbelieving companions was exchanged for that of believers — all external objects and occupations which might have distracted his attention, were excluded by the state of his sight and health; and his mind, thus shut in upon itself, became gradually 'prepared,' under the influence of these salutary circumstances, for the reception of the truth. Three years before, Mr. SCOTT would have made no impression upon him; not that I mean to depreciate Mr. SCOTT, for I know no author more truly sound and scriptural; but where 'the deaf adder stoppeth her ears,' it is in vain for 'the charmer to charm ever so wisely.'

"The Apostle says, 'Put off the old man,' and 'put on the new man, which after Christ is created unto holiness,' &c.; and the allusion is apt to mislead us into an idea, that this saving change is to be effected as speedily and as readily as a change of garments. But that this is not his meaning his writings abundantly testify; for renovation of heart and life is spoken of as being progressive: the established habits, especially, of 'the old man,' cleave long to the new; and as intellectual habits are of all others perhaps the most difficult to shake off, it seems but natural to expect that those who have once been unbelievers should long continue to be harassed by doubts and unbelief; since old indulged trains of thought will be constantly recurring to the mind, and leading to their former inferences. But then, we all have our peculiar conflicts and trials—'our besetting sins;' we are all assured, at our first setting out, that 'this is not our rest;' we are no where given to understand that our spiritual life is to be one of indolence, and ease, and unmixed comfort; it is, on the contrary, always represented as 'a race,' 'a warfare,' 'a pilgrimage;'—every metaphor implies that progress is expected, and that progress cannot be made without labour, and exertion, and difficulty. The Christian, too, has not that support which other men derive from the inflation of pride and self-complacency — he is of ' a broken and contrite spirit ' — he mourns continually under a sense of his remaining sins and infirmities. But what then? he has ' joys which the world knows not of,' which *it* ' can neither give nor take away;' he has the exhilarating assurance, ' Blessed are they that' thus ' mourn, for they shall be comforted;' he has ' exceeding great and precious promises;' he realises the seeming paradox of the Apostle, ' sorrowful, yet alway rejoicing :' and he would not exchange his sorrows for all that the world can offer him, because he knows that these ' light afflictions, which are but for a moment, will work for him a far more exceeding and eternal weight of glory;' he reckons that ' the sufferings of this present time are not worthy to be compared to the glory that shall be revealed.' Partakers of the same grace, heirs of the same promises, and the same glory, Christians have a bond of union far beyond that of any common friendship," &c.

Thus ended the pages which have been already laid before the public in another form. They were originally written without any view to the notice soon taken of them, or to publicity at all, excepting as the account of the facts might be thought likely to be useful to others by the much respected clergyman to whose hands, at his desire, it was conveyed, as matter for his farther preparation, and with the particular request that, if judged worthy of publication, the narrative might be given in the third person. The different course which ensued, in regard both to that narrative and to the confidential letters from which the two latter transcripts have been taken, is now of little importance. One object only is here in view, to give a faithful account of all that is known concerning Dr. BATEMAN, by his nearest connections and friends. With that, the duty they owed to him and to the public is fulfilled. All the material particulars of his life have been related; and the principal features of his character have been represented with as much care as solicitude for the truth, and affection for his memory, could supply.

Such a life is not, in the ordinary sense of the word, eventful. Yet both to those who are and those who are not aware of the importance of early principles and habits, whether of good or evil; and to those who are and those who are not interested in contemplating the developement of character, it may alike furnish matter for useful and not unpleasing reflection. For neither the professional nor the moral course here described was one of every day. In either aspect there was enough to leave a deep impression on those who were sufficiently near to witness it; and a corresponding anxiety, that others also should enjoy the means thus given to them of considering the example itself, and the sentiments to which it seemed so naturally to lead, that it would have been as difficult to suppress them as to obtrude any which do not in some way belong to it. Biography, if but a bare and naked detail of facts, can be but of little use. Its proper method would appear to be to deliver those facts with scrupulous fidelity, as in some sort public property, and along with them such observations as flow spontaneously, as it were, out of their very nature and substance. The application of the example, or of the sentiments which it has thus suggested to such as " took sweet counsel with him," and to whom his memory is as a part of themselves; the application of either to the case or the mind of the reader is business for his own thought and care. It is the duty of the writer to provide for him conscientiously the full use of whatsoever means he can; the rest must be left, without taking farther liberty, to himself.

The prevalence of scepticism among those whose time and talents are devoted to the acquisition of an intimate acquaintance with the structure and economy of the human frame, in which are displayed so many proofs of benevolence and design, has been apprehended by others before Dr. BATEMAN. And it has been thought strange besides, that those who witness, more perhaps than any other individuals, the influence of religion under the most trying difficulties of life, should be insensible to its importance, or hesitate to inquire into the grounds on which its truth is established. It is to be hoped that many more than are heard of, or are imagined, in the medical world, do indeed draw those conclusions from their peculiar opportunities and advantages; and live in those principles, the rejection of which is so naturally a matter of astonishment to others. Very illustrious examples are not wanting to prove, from time to time, that the knowledge of anatomy may indeed inspire religious sentiments. The inferences which the celebrated HARVEY drew from his researches, and the acknowledged piety of SYDENHAM, of BOERHAAVE, and of HALLER, are solid testimonies in favour of those great men. The general spirit breathing through the annual orations of Sir JOHN PRINGLE before the Royal Society, is to the same salutary effect. The religious character of Mr. HEY, throughout his long and useful life, demonstrates, that neither the preliminary studies, nor the most diligent exercise of the practical duties of the medical profession, is inconsistent with the steadiest and most devoted attachment to the doctrines of the Bible. And Dr. BAILLIE, whose name is too fresh in our affections to be reverted to on any occasion lightly, was earnest in declaring his powerful mind against infidelity. The American student, who once drew forth at his table an eager expression of his belief in the Christian doctrine of future retribution, and of the necessity of that retribution to human nature, may now perhaps remember his admirable master with the more veneration for the emphasis and warmth of that striking and very characteristic moment. To the same purport may be adduced the following passage, as a pleasing evidence of the sentiments suggested to a medical writer directly by his subject. In treating of the preservatives against the inordinate fear of death, the late ingenious Dr. REID observes, in his Essay on *Hypochondriasis,* "The Christian is still more highly privileged. His eye, happily invigorated by faith, is able to penetrate the thick mist which hangs over the tomb, and which to our unassisted sight intercepts any farther prospect. The light of Divine Revelation is, after all, the only light which can effectually disperse the gloom of a sick chamber, and irradiate even the countenance of death."

To these, and, wheresoever they can be found, to all substantial evidences of religious belief, it is comfortable to turn. Whatever be the tendency of their early studies, medical practitioners are placed in particular circumstances. They have frequently but little opportunity for much reading out of their own professional subjects; and the world, with which they are conversant, does not supply the deficiency. Hence, in the anxious discharge of the urgent duties of every day and every hour, they are liable to be tempted farther and farther away from any close examination of the question of Revelation. But there is a sufficient provision for all men; and to them it is suited with a peculiar felicity. The Bible may accompany them in all their movements; and the Bible is enough. Neither other books, of whatsoever merit, nor the world when most unexceptionable, can instruct them in this knowledge. With the Bible rightly sought into, they cannot fail; for, to use the words of LOCKE, " it has God for its author, truth, without any mixture of error, for its subject, and salvation for its end." But without it, whatever may be their advantages besides, they may fall into the same distress as came upon the excellent LINACRE, a name deservedly dear to the medical history of ENGLAND, and of whom " a remarkable anecdote," says Doctor AIKIN, "is told by Sir JOHN CHEKE. He relates, that LINACRE, a little before his death, when worn out with sickness and fatigues, first began to read the New Testament; and that when he had perused the fifth, sixth, and seventh chapters of St. Matthew, he threw the book from him with great violence, passionately exclaiming, " Either this is not the Gospel, or we are not Christians!" So new to the learning of the venerable Founder of the College of Physicians, at the age of more than threescore years, the friend of Dean COLET, of ERASMUS, of MELANCTHON, was the light which then flashed upon him!

Some very important considerations present themselves here. The very first principle in *philosophy* is to take nothing upon authority. Nothing is to be admitted but facts. The facts are to be proved; and the inductions from them are to be such as cannot be disputed. Whatsoever calls itself philosophy must come to us on these conditions; otherwise we decline to listen to it altogether. And unquestionably there can be no true philosophy on any other terms; that is to say, there can be no dependence on any thing averred by man to man, of himself, but as he *proves* what he declares for fact to be such; and so reasons upon that fact, that no other reasoning can be brought against him. The extreme severity of this test is unavoidable. Its necessity lies in the very constitution of our nature. It must be so because our faculties are limited, and we can find out nothing by ourselves, so as to be sure of it, in any other manner. Nothing else, in a word, is *knowledge*. And hence the modesty and the humility of every philosopher, properly so called. He does not take upon him to affirm the smallest matter, but as he is able to demonstrate it, for he knows that he has no right so to presume.

But "*faith* is the substance of things hoped for, the evidence of things not seen." In faith, therefore, authority is every thing; and our only inquiry here is into the evidences of the authority itself, not of the things which that authority announces. They are to be taken implicitly as they are delivered. The concern of *philosophy* is with this world, which is seen; that of *faith*, with the world which is not seen. In philosophy, man is called upon at every step (such does he find his power of apprehension and his capacity to be) to rejoice and be thankful, with an " understanding heart," that he has been made only " a little lower than the angels." In faith, he meets with things which even " the angels desire to look into." He has been created with faculties sufficient for his purposes on this earth: but beyond it, " knowledge is too wonderful and excellent for him, he cannot attain unto it." The difference would seem to be of easy comprehension; to be such as suits the condition we see ourselves to be actually in here, and the great change which Revelation proclaims to be its consequence. There is nothing in it at variance from that analogy which may be traced in all we have to do with. But there *is* this difference. We have been apprised of it; and therefore, when we turn from philosophy, and prepare to address ourselves to the subject of Revelation, it behoves us to bear it in mind. We must leave the philosophical principle to the province in which, being all we needed, it has served us so well; and proceed with an absolute submission of the understanding to matters which, although they may best exercise the highest, are yet so placed in respect to it as to be altogether unapproachable by its own unassisted powers.

And in this requirement there is nothing unreasonable. We are daily acting upon a similar principle in our common earthly concerns. If we wish to become acquainted with the circumstances of a country which we have not seen, we are satisfied to depend upon the authority of a witness of approved veracity.

Yet it may easily happen that this difference between the objects of philosophy and those of faith, essential as it is, may be overlooked in the ardent prosecution of knowledge; or that its practical consequences may not be practically admitted; so that the inquirer after truth, seeking it by instruments intended only for the discovery of its inferior forms, falls into the capital error of concluding against its most glorious manifestations, because these cannot from their nature be so apprehended: as if a man, whose telescope had brought a beautiful mid-day landscape home to his delighted eye in all its perfection, should discredit an authentic description of " a better country," because either night or distance denied him the sight of it through the very same glass!

There is another and a still greater difficulty in the way of scientific men to religion. It arises indeed out of the former; but in itself it probably exceeds even that, in the tenacity with which it resists dislodgement, inasmuch as it concerns the temper rather than the understanding.

The philosopher calls no one master; he seeks and judges for himself. The Christian is a *disciple*. The prime requisite to religious belief is an entire surrender of the whole mind, to be taught even as a little child; nay, a perpetual fervent desire that there may be an end with it for ever of every thought of its own, and of all teaching, save only of " the wisdom which is from above." With this there is no dispute. It is perfect, and as such must be received, even as it has been given.

But to a mind long habituated to a jealous scrutiny of every object of its examination, and that as a matter not less of duty than necessity, in order that nothing be admitted there, which, from whatsoever intellect it proceeded, itself is unequal to take in, every demand of subjection is felt as an unjust invasion of the proper " dignity of human nature." The will is gradually involved. Instead of the humble frame of a learner, a sentiment of equality of right, if not of attainment, is fixed in the breast; and to every admonition to an acknowledgment of sovereignty, the characteristic feeling of the *republic* of letters rises, if not to an open rejection of all interference, at least to a degree which excludes any benefit from the gracious offer of instruction. The situation of a philosophic mind in respect to religion, is therefore peculiar. Trained in a scrupulous particularity, the understanding is shocked, as if something unreasonable were required of it; and violence is done to the most natural of all human feelings when such a mind, perhaps of the finest constitution, is told to be satisfied in a manner the very reverse of every thing it has hitherto considered to be indispensable to satisfaction, and in this matter to make no account of itself any more for ever. But there is no alternative. The understanding must submit to authority; and the will must submit to authority; or there can be no progress in religion, for there can be no beginning.

These considerations, if well founded, may help to explain the disinclination to religious subjects which is often imputed to men of science; and they suggest a method of treating them, with a view to the conviction of such persons, more direct than that which might otherwise be employed. For would it not promise more success to take up the cause at once on its own principles, than to deal with it after a manner which implies that it rests on similar proofs to those of any ordinary matter of demonstration? To keep strictly, when convinced ourselves, to the plain assertion of our satisfaction, and of the *scriptural* grounds of our convincement? The moment we travel out of these, we are in hazard. For the privilege of comprehending the universal system of things is not here vouchsafed to us; and although our reason and knowledge, wisely applied, may prove invaluable auxiliaries, they are not to be depended upon as the sole means of conversion. Very judicious and experienced divines have observed that they have conquered objections soonest, and most effectually, by simply urging the doctrines of the Bible, and standing fast to their office of declaring "the whole counsel of God." It is not given to man to understand mysteries; and it is in vain for him to endeavour to make them less mysterious. The attempt, if it does not entangle, at the best wastes some portion of the precious opportunity which might be spent upon the heavenly oracles themselves. An opposite mode of proceeding may keep down, too, in some measure, the pride incident alike to him who teaches, and him who is to be taught; or rather, which is so inherent in our common nature, that unless each shall submit to renounce his self-dependence, both may be the worse rather than the better for beginning.

It is, moreover, remarkable that the arguments, which have most disquieted unbelievers of honest minds, or which have been most pertinaciously pressed by others, do no longer offend the convert, although, agreeably to the supposition of this suggestion, no answer to them has been, nor indeed could have been, given to him. Dr. BATEMAN, although he had been accustomed to recur anxiously to certain philosophical difficulties on all previous occasions of religious discussion, appeared never to think of them again after his conversion. Yet those difficulties, such as they had been, were difficulties still. No explanation had come to him of any of his former questions; yet, notwithstanding his being equally aware that they were questions still, he was satisfied and happy. He had never been more competent at any period, never better disposed, to the consideration of scientific subjects, than during the last year of his life; but having been led to view those of a religious nature in their own true light, his philosophical doubts troubled him no more.

The benefits which characters above the common level of mankind diffuse around them in their day, are better understood as well as felt when their course is concluded. "De mortuis nil nisi *verum*" is the sacred obligation of those who undertake the task of biography; for their main business is to put others in possession of what they themselves know. They are bound both to state and to withhold only in such a manner as that the public shall have all the requisite means of judging for themselves. It is not their part to settle the final value either of the works or the character they describe. But although the just province of biography be expressed in that brief maxim, the feelings of mankind tend rather to its original text, "Nil nisi *bonum*." Whatever was of no importance to the great business of life we seldom think of. Whatever was otherwise than we could have wished, we regard with a tenderness very different from that sharp comparison with which we were prone to remark upon our neighbour while he walked to and fro among ourselves. We muse rather, and we speak, when that great change has passed upon him which makes " the place that knew him to know him no more," of his virtues, the thought of which in our fondest moments never touched us as it does now. Our whole idea of his departed image falls imperceptibly into that affecting form which the sculptor, as he delivers his marble from its imperfections, and aims purposely at excellence, sets up for unqualified admiration. Nor is such a bias of humanity inconsistent with the strictest fidelity. In our retrospect of a long journey the memory loves chiefly to dwell upon a few favourite spots; but every stage of the scene imprinted its picture as we passed, and contributed unconsciously to the general impression left upon the mind, so as to temper, by the sequence and relative connection of all its parts, the pleasure with which we look back upon it and recommend the same course to others. The hard insensibility of systematic criticism, or a habit or judging by artificial rules, may give a different clue to the estimate of character. But nature and charity do justice better than either: and to these, as they prevail in unsophisticated minds, the foregoing account is now committed. Its purpose is to show by what means a man beloved by his friends won and held fast possession of their esteem and confidence; the methods by which he rose early in life to eminence as a physician; and the circumstances which enabled him, in the height of every advantage which he desired in this world, to take leave of all its delights with joy and thankfulness. The facts which have been detailed are from the beginning simple, and of direct application to the business of life, in all its interests, both temporal and eternal, not matters of distant and doubtful contemplation. They come therefore within the cognisance of every judgment which exercises its own proper liberty, and need no painful solicitation of the understanding or the heart. For their own worth, not any ability with which they might have been set forth, must determine the measure of the public attention which they may gain.

Dr. BATEMAN was an only son; and was in early youth deprived of his father, a man of superior mind, and well to be remembered as one of " the excellent of the earth." How much he might owe to paternal instructions and watchfulness cannot be known. But it is certain that impressions may be instilled into the mind, and dispositions for good, or for evil, as soon as any other impressions; and that, besides direct admonitions and instructions, suited to an opening capacity, even the countenance and the voice of such a parent must influence the expanding character of his child. To say here with how perfect an affection, and how rare a discretion that great loss was compensated, and to the last moment of his life supplied, would be doing too certain a violence to a tenderness, which from its very nature shrinks from every eye but that of its object, were it not a duty to point out every probable source of good. For that the steady integrity of Dr. BATEMAN's general conduct, and his faithful discharge of every professional duty, were intimately connected with his exemplary filial reverence, will be readily apprehended by any who are qualified to reflect on that best foundation of moral principle. And if any encouragement were wanting to diligence and perseverance in early religious instruction, the remarkable change which was finally wrought upon him might be safely adduced with that view. For Dr. BATEMAN had never lost entirely that benefit of such care without which the hope of conversion must have been still less. He had never spoken of religion, nor of religious characters, with levity. In whatsoever company he might hear them treated irreverently, his own tongue was not known to join in the licence. On the contrary, such language always evidently gave him offence and pain. Neither did he make unbelief a plea for immorality nor indecorum of any kind. While there was least of the religious principle, much of the *moral* good remained. That awe for religion which became one of the first sentiments and feelings of his childhood, saved him afterward in the most trying circumstances from more vicious consequences of unbelief, and afforded a secret basis for the ultimate triumph of truth. The seed had been planted in the seed-time; and with many tears had it been watered; and in his own good season it pleased God to " give the increase." Duties are imperative things. It is a duty to " train up a child in the way he should go." And *prayer* is a duty. For we " ought always to pray, and not to faint." Happy the mother of whom it may thus be said that " she openeth her mouth with wisdom, and in her tongue is the law of kindness;" for " her children arise up, and call her blessed!"

Very precious also are the fruits of early parental attention to the cultivation of the affections. For these require as much care as principles. The counterparts of both, the evil propensities, and the bad passions of our nature, exhibit their first motions with the earliest mental apprehensions: and surely it is then, therefore, that the office of watching and checking them should be commenced. But in no part of the momentous business of education is this vigilance more indispensable than in regard to the domestic affections. For unless the selfish principle be continually repressed, they are so enfeebled by its urgent importunities as to be gradually absorbed in it. The contact between brothers and sisters is so close, the collision so frequent, that, as in other cases, to prevent war, no means of preserving peace must be neglected. The grand point is not to keep down disorder by mere constraint, howsoever well devised; but by the infusion of counteracting good principles and kind feelings, and the cherishing of these to the utmost, at all times and in all possible ways. The affections are no more to be trusted to themselves than the tenderest plants. These we nurse up, and keep from all violence, or they die. And so too must it be with those far tenderer moral germs, which have been provided for the best benefits, and the most exquisite gratifications of our maturer days; nay, are the roots, from whence are to spring up all that is to stamp the character for ever, and thus essentially to influence the solemn question, whether eternity shall be inconceivably happy or miserable. For with the birth of the child commences a being which is to have no end, a capacity for affection, which is, in fact, the only capacity for happiness; a right or a wrong direction of that power of the soul, determining the difference between happiness and misery; between Heaven, therefore, and its awful contrast! In this view, how momentous is the duty of the parent and the tutor to look with all diligence to whatsoever, in any way, involves moral feelings, actions, and habits! It is by perverted affections that sensibility is extinguished, and not by advancing age (as is so commonly supposed); for age only acts by strengthening habits, and therefore confirms and expands the benevolent affections as surely as it rivets the selfish. In this great particular, then, as in every other, " train up a child in the way he should go, and when he is old he will not depart from it!" And what is there, indeed, in this sublunary scene which does not in like manner demand our best diligence in order to its perfection? Do we expect intellectual improvement of any kind without labour? That the memory, for example, should be exact, or the taste refined, without constant pains to exercise the one and enlighten the other? Why shall we leave faculties of more importance than all besides to their own course, as if a fear for them were unnatural to justify any care but about their extreme excesses? To them, indeed, we must attend; or they would soon grow too vehement and too mischievous to be borne. But the remedies required on such emergencies are themselves also extreme; so that matters, instead of being made better by them, are not seldom left in reality worse. What evil of any other description do we see springing up, and permit to get a head of us, before we interfere? Do we wait for the embers to burst into a conflagration? What else, among all the varieties of human offence, would we not fain "nip in the bud?" and that for the best of all reasons, that it must be done then, or perhaps never done effectually. How lamentable to stand by, and witness the little ebullitions of childish envy, and malice, and rage, and selfishness, without an effort to extinguish them, seeing that these must in so short a time otherwise break out with the fearful strength of full-grown vices! Time only developes the rudiments of the embryo. What is now so minute as to be scarcely perceived, will by and by be too big for our grasp: —

"Non Hydra secto corpore firmior
Vinci dolentem crevit in Herculem!"

In a letter, in which some recent discussion of the subject of moral character is adverted to by Dr. BATEMAN, he too observes, in his accustomed manner of just reflection on whatsoever it fell in his way to think of, " we ought to consider the danger of allowing *self-love* to receive its gratifications unrestrained, although the only means of demanding them be cries and frets, before language is formed for the purpose. Habit strengthens its claims; and at length, where self-denial has never been taught by precept and example, nor enforced by command, unhappiness is the consequence where the object cannot be obtained, or vice the means resorted to for procuring it, where the laws of justice and religion forbid it to be demanded. The *child* that has not been taught to consider the comforts and happiness of its play-fellows, will never grow into a *man* of justice, mercy, and benevolence. For 'men are but children of a larger growth;' and although Reason may in them *discover* that the feelings are selfish and malevolent, she never yet could alter their tendency:—

"Video meliora, proboque,
　Deteriora sequor!"

says Virgil. In all our actions, (by which character is known,) where our own interest is concerned, the feelings are the very guides and leaders of reason; and, therefore, it is evident how much character depends on the early cultivation of the passions. And how extensive also, and all-powerful is the effect of early association! Nothing is, to me, more interesting than the study of man; whether I examine his structure and functions, as part of my own profession, or the history of his intellect and passions, by which the world is ruled, by which empires have risen or decayed, by which the earth itself, and its elements, have been made subservient to his happiness; and on which all the actions of individuals and society depend."

This difference there is, however, between natural and moral progression, that the former proceeds by laws which admit of no improvement from human hands; the latter is only to be accomplished by the subjugation of a principle coeval and interwoven with its very existence. It is impossible to be aware of moral evil too soon; to aim at it with too determined an hostility; to be too uncompromising with it at any stage of its appearance. The particular weapons with which we contend against it may be, from time to time, matter for consideration: but from first to last there can be no truce nor peace with it. In any shape, and with whatsoever force it comes, there is no safety but in war, and that in the old settled spirit of extermination itself, "*Delenda est Carthago!*"

In the cultivation of the affections of the young, this clearing of the soil is an essential preliminary. For if that be pre-occupied with wrong dispositions, above all, if it be deeply impregnated with that pride which the admirable MILNER calls " the essence of the fall," and which is in fact the foul spring of every thing wrong within us, there can be little room for the expansion of better feelings, although they do for a moment now and then put forth a flattering show. But when this great, and no doubt difficult task, is faithfully and wisely performed, then, full play being so given to all innocent emotions and tender affections, it may, indeed, be seen with how large a bounty the heart is by nature framed. So richly will it be found endowed with every lovely quality, that this preparation alone may perhaps lead to an inestimable superiority of character; to a freedom from selfishness, and a proportionate interest in the enjoyments of others, which without it is not to be expected. Yet that preparation is neither all which is practicable; nor the principal part of the duty. As in every other moral requirement, we are not to stop at a negative advantage, but to follow up our endeavours for positive good. To complete —

> " the fairer forms
> That cultivation glories in,"

must be superadded an active and unremitted inculcation of the apostolic precept, " Be ye kind one to another; tender-hearted, forgiving one another;" and of the great commandment, " That ye love one another." Affection must be grounded on principle; and principle must be scriptural, and scripturally enforced, " in meekness instructing those that oppose themselves."

How pleasant the sight of a house so ruled! and its promise of future happiness and honour to such as have thus fulfilled the most sacred of all human obligations, must indeed be —

"The comfort of a reasonable joy!"

For, in default of the domestic affections, whence are to come the social! Much harm in these things has arisen, no doubt, from the misuse of the commonest of all words. We say that a child has been out of *temper;* that his temper is wrong: and temper we consider a venial evil; rather as a misfortune than a fault. We give it a reproof, perhaps, as it passes. But " it was his temper;" and there, unless it has caused us more than usual trouble, our concern ends. Yet, from the beginning of the Bible to the end, it is remarkable that there is no such word. The Bible is the word of truth; and gives to every thing, therefore, its true name; and of all the contrivances of the human heart to elude its searching scrutiny, and its strict commands, none perhaps has been so effectual as this of inventing soft, and specious, and qualifying terms, under covert of which sin may pass unreproved, and almost unnoticed. Every variety of what we are accustomed to call *temper* is forbidden in Scripture under its true form and name; and will be found to be some shade or degree of pride, envy, anger, revenge, covetousness, selfishness, malice; of some of those evil passions which it is the great business of religion and of education to repress and eradicate; and which we can never hope to subdue in ourselves, or in others, if we do not see them in their true colours, and call them by their right names. The obvious effect of the use of a milder or too general term is to dilute the sense of the evil. If we would employ any other single word as an equivalent for *temper* we must say *the heart*, taking with us the account of the heart, which we find in the Bible, for there, nothing relating to it, or to what we have to desire or to do with it, is ever made a light matter.

Human nature is the same in all ages. Opinions and habits vary. The fashion of the present times is to encourage an early feeling of freedom and independence. It seems to be thought better that the boy should not wait to grow into a man, nor the girl into a woman; but that they should announce themselves to be men and women as soon as they please. It was not so formerly. But in that revolution which is said to take place, from time to time, in opinions as well as in all other human matters, it is possible that reason may be found hereafter to go back, even to what we use ourselves to call " the dark ages ;" a mine, it may be remarked by the way, which, however wearisome it may seem to dig into, would not seldom repay the toil of exploring it with far better metal than many a more boasted one. Of St. NICHOLAS it is said, in old an legend concerning boy-bishops, as they were called, (boys, therefore, were then made much of, it would seem, in proportion to such qualities,) " This meekness and simplicity, the proper virtues of children, he maintained from his childhood as long as he lived." And surely, unless there be this meekness and simplicity in childhood, little is to be looked for of moderation, justice, or the love of truth, afterward: or of much real regard to the golden rule, "Whatsoever ye would that men should do unto you, do ye also unto them." "Charity begins at home." The proverb may be converted to a better use than that to which it is so familiarly applied; and may, on the contrary, be made a perpetual admonition both to tutor and pupil against the encouragement of that selfishness, which is the great bane of every worthy hope. Youth is but the unfolding of childhood, and maturity the confirmation of every antecedent process. The pride which refuses subordination to any moral standard but that of the world, and which is in fact its own standard, was perhaps a natural part of such a character as the ancient Roman. But if we look to the Bible for our rule, this must be melted into that precious spirit which is said to be "the bond of perfectness."

Assuredly, too, it is in this way that firmness of character also, fortitude, and all the severer virtues, are best to be secured; for their proper basis is in the same renunciation of selfishness and vanity.

With an attachment to his family, equally warm and rational, Dr. BATEMAN was thoroughly imbued. It " grew with his growth and strengthened with his strength:" and after securing to him a source of pure enjoyment, in the singularly regular correspondence which has been before mentioned, and the consciousness of the affection felt for him, through the many years in which his actual intercourse with them was only at distant intervals and for very short seasons, proved finally the greatest blessing to him. Of that devotedness to him, which his long and distressing illnesses called forth, he was duly sensible. He knew indeed, that no care, no watchings, no assiduities, day after day, and night after night, of which nature was capable, were spared; but that they were still rendered with all the heart, and all the strength. And besides this utmost exertion of bodily attention, that not a thought nor a feeling, at work within him, which could be guessed, was for a moment slighted. He knew that even such of his sentiments as kept up an inexpressible anxiety, as were accompanied with a fear which could hardly sleep — he knew that even these were regarded also with the same sisterly tenderness; that the same compassion and solicitude were tremblingly alive for his body and soul. The pleasures of his childhood, the higher gratifications of youth, and the more intellectual interchange of sentiment and affection which had delighted his riper years, had long made that tenderness, as it were, an essential part of his daily comforts; and in the infinite goodness of the infinitely wise God, it was made the blessed instrument of his conversion to the faith of the ever-glorious Gospel, in a day when all earthly hope had well nigh disappeared. It is material to repeat, that it was especially through the exercise of this tenderness that the wonderful change appeared to be brought about. Had that been less than it was, or had the dependence on any ability of argument been greater, a different course would unavoidably have been taken. An anxiety more dreadful from its very nature than any other can be, an apprehension of imminent peril of the last extremity, would have vented itself more in every way than in that silent and continual prayer, which, after so many years of care to keep back no part of personal profession from his eye or his ear, was alone to be looked to. He knew all that passed in the heart at his bedside; for to have concealed its distress was not possible; nor, had it been so, would it have been deemed allowable. More might have offended; and the work was effected without.

The difficulty likely to be felt in a similar situation is, that it may be wrong not to say every awakening word, to use every argument which can be thought of. No rule is here presumptuously laid down for others. Principle and conscience must direct. In this remarkable instance there was no want of a clear reciprocal understanding. No customary religious observances were intermitted on account of his presence, whether in health, or in sickness; and it is hardly probable, that even the sight of a happy family of children, so trained, should be entirely without effect upon his susceptible feelings. He delighted in their talents and attainments, as well as their dispositions; for he knew them all to be above mediocrity. And he knew also in what " nurture and admonition" they were governed; and what was their morning and their evening song. The particular circumstances of the case, and the character of the individual concerned, are to be deliberately weighed wheresoever such an occasion exists for anxiety; or its momentous object may be frustrated by the very means taken to relieve it. The walk and conversation he so witnessed were the only arguments addressed to Dr. BATEMAN until a way was graciously made for more direct application to his mind and conscience. These he could not mistake; and assured of this, the heart, full as it was, could not have brought itself to any other expression of its care than that which, although silent, could neither be unobserved nor misinterpreted. The great point in all cases would seem to be, that, whatsoever is done, there should not be too busy an interference: and perhaps the surest check to this lies in the real desire for the object, to the utter exclusion of all self-importance in its accomplishment. In such a frame we shall be less intent upon argument than consistency. Where we apprehend impatience, we shall strive to be ourselves patient; and in the just and steady exercise of our own liberty, we shall deal with gentleness and respect toward that which as rightfully belongs to all others. For " the end of the commandment is charity out of a pure heart, and of a good conscience, and of faith unfeigned."

By his friends, in the profession and out of it, Dr. BATEMAN was held in uniform and high regard. It was not the admiration of talent alone which sustained so permanent and so strong a feeling. They knew, likewise, and valued, the sincere and steady sentiments of attachment by which he was himself actuated. In the ordinary intercourse of society, his varied attainments, and simplicity of manner, rendered him an acceptable companion. His unimpeached integrity was a still more solid ground for that confidence on which alone more intimate acquaintance can satisfactorily rest.

As a member of the public polity, his opinions were in favour of the existing order and constitution of the state, and on the side of the government of his country. These he would support with much animation, and force of reasoning, occasionally enlivening the argument with sallies of humour or raillery. But political differences never led him to personal estrangement; nor did his zeal for what he considered the public good, lessen his warmth of private friendship.

The extraordinary diligence with which he pursued his studies has been already noticed, as well as the unwearied assiduity which he afterward displayed, and which gave the character and impress of utility to all he undertook. His early and habitual love of study had stored his mind with all that ancient and modern medicine could provide of any useful purport. He was well qualified, therefore, for the task on which he entered, of writing the medical articles for the Cyclopædia. But although his mind was so thoroughly prepared, and that he composed with such facility, he omitted no means to render himself more perfectly familiar with his sub-

ject before he committed his thoughts to paper;
"Nil actum reputans, dum quid superesset agendum."

The value of Dr. BATEMAN's publications has been fully proved by the reception given to them by the medical world. His SYNOPSIS has already passed through several large editions at home, besides its translations into the foreign languages which have been mentioned. And the utility of his larger work, the "DELINEATIONS," appears also to be duly appreciated. His "TREATISE ON FEVER" has reached a second edition, and may be strongly recommended to those who wish to possess a practical view of that important subject, bearing in mind that Dr. BATEMAN himself modified his opinions and practice by the results of observation; and that it is equally the duty of all who may consult it as their guide, to make a careful investigation of the circumstances before they adopt any particular treatment, under the varying character assumed by different epidemics. The reports on the diseases of the metropolis have also been referred to. They had been first sent, as they were drawn up through ten successive years, to the Edinburgh Medical and Surgical Journal. For the spirit of acute and accurate observation which they evinced, Dr. BATEMAN was indebted not only to the vigour and precision of his own mind, but to the early bent given to it, and probably in no inconsiderable degree, by the opportunities he enjoyed of witnessing the caution and sagacity which characterised the researches of Dr. WILLAN. Besides the uniform bearing of these reports to what is practically useful, they are not less distinguished by an enlightened and active benevolence, as may be presently seen, wheresoever the question of Vaccination or any topic of essential interest to the community is the subject of discussion. For Vaccination indeed he was an able and a consistent advocate; and drew up an excellent paper on this important subject for the first volume of the Philanthropist.

As an author, Dr. BATEMAN is remarkable for the clearness and unaffected style of his composition; and for the power which he possessed of discriminating truth amidst conflicting testimonies. The account of *Elephantiasis*, contained in his Synopsis, is a strong illustration of this faculty. And in Mr. ROBINSON's paper in the tenth volume of the Medico-Chirurgical Transactions, we have the testimony of a writer who has enjoyed very considerable opportunities of studying that remarkable disease in India, in confirmation of Dr. BATEMAN's accuracy in describing it.

His intercourse with his professional brethren was conducted in the same spirit which characterised every other part of his behaviour. He was an honest man; and in discharging his own duty every where to the best of his ability, never directly or indirectly defrauded another of his claims, bearing in remembrance often, besides his natural desire to do right, the honourable manner in which he was wont to say his former master, Dr. BAILLIE, invariably treated him when called in consultation to his patients. On such occasions, he was fond of repeating, he always found that he stood better himself with the patient and his friends than before. His friends therefore loved him, and his professional acquaintances honoured him. And the estimation in which his services were held at the benevolent institutions to which they were dedicated, was testified by repeated votes of thanks, the compliments of which he well merited. To these substantial proofs of the good opinion of all who knew him, his simple integrity, love of truth, and steady obedience to every demand of duty, as they never wore in any degree an artificial appearance, but were the unstudied manifestations of his real character, naturally conducted him. And here it can hardly be wrong to record a testimony to his professional care and humanity from a quarter seldom alluded to in a manner to reflect much honour upon human nature, since it exhibits a sense of justice, and a capacity of feeling there, which do not admit of any sinister interpretation. Many of his Dispensary patients resided in the worst parts of St. Giles's; and thither it was his business to follow them. The scenes he had thus to traverse were often as fearful as they were distressing; but he did his duty to his patients; and even in that extreme depth of depravity there were never wanting some to do theirs to him. For the wretched people knew the value of his visits, and fierce as they were, it was common for the first who caught sight of him, as he entered their appalling precincts, to step forward for the purpose of protecting and conducting "the Doctor!" to the sick room.* Happy the country, whose charities are so administered! — whose servants are thus faithful to their trust, howsoever difficult or revolting; and the most abject of whose inmates involuntarily so testify to the praise of both! Let no man, while he labours in such a calling as he ought, for a moment doubt of his sufficient reward! It may not come to him in the shape he expects, or would choose; but come it will, if he honestly merits it; and surely in the form for which he may be above all most thankful, if, as in

* A friend who was once walking through the streets with him, will not soon forget the expression which lighted up the countenance of a labourer, who, on suddenly meeting them, exclaimed, "God bless you, Sir! God bless your Honour!" On Dr. Bateman being asked who the poor man was, he said he did not recollect, but did not doubt he had been a patient at the Fever House or the Dispensary, it being very common for such greetings to happen to him from his Irish patients there.

this instance, while he is made the instrument of healing the diseases, it is given him also to soften the hearts of the most hopeless of his kind!

His zeal for the advancement of knowledge was evinced by the warm interest he took in the various societies with which he was connected, and of which he was an efficient and much valued associate. In Edinburgh he had thus gained a place among the most worthy of his fellow-students: and on coming to London, he joined the Medical Society in Bolt Court. He was also a fellow of the Linnæan Society; but resigned his seat on leaving London in 1819. He was a member too of the Academical Society: and on the resignation of its first President, likewise a distinguished physician, Dr. BATEMAN was called to the chair, and reelected through several sessions; as long indeed as he was able to devote sufficient time to the duties of the office. On the foundation of the Medical and Chirurgical Society of London, he took an active part in its proceedings. And the character which he had established for a profound knowledge of medical literature led to his being appointed its librarian, a post not of mere distinction, but attended with considerable labour in assisting to form the valuable collection of books which that very respectable society possesses; and to arrange its catalogue for publication.

Dr. BATEMAN was thus an eminent and an useful man "in his day and generation." His career was interrupted at its height, and when he had most to expect from emolument and fame. After the unexpected amendment which took place in his health during the summer of 1820, it was proposed to him by a medical friend whom he greatly respected, that he should in the ensuing winter fix himself in York; and this being the field he had originally looked to, he acceded to the scheme with much satisfaction. Yet he often felt a dread of returning to an intercourse with the world, lest he should fall in any degree under the influence it formerly had over him. And when the season he had thought of for the execution of this plan approached, and he found himself gradually sinking into a state of debility which shut out all expectation that he could ever again be equal to the fatigues of practice, he sometimes expressed the most devout and lively thankfulness that the matter was so determined for him, saying how much rather he would choose his present weakness than such a state of health as would have required him to return into the world. "So far," were his own words in a letter written at this date, "from there being any risk, of which you intimated some apprehension, that I may become too much smitten with the world, it seems to me that a continuance of the seclusion I have been in for some time, added to my want of bodily alertness, together with the train of reading we have been upon, would be in danger of inducing such a total indifference to the turmoil of gain and pleasure, in which the multitude are so exclusively engaged, as to repress even those exertions which duty requires while we are here; so unimportant do all pursuits and gratifications now seem to me, which I once thought were all that constituted the value of existence. That sudden stay to my fair progress to fame and fortune, which I formerly thought so hard, I now deem the greatest blessing of a kind providence, and would not exchange one hour of that 'peace which passeth all understanding' for years of what is past."

He was at this time going through MILNER's Church History, which was read to him. The accounts given in that masterly work of the Christian converts from paganism, who first set the example of quitting society to devote their lives to the worship of God in solitary caves and deserts, led him to observe that this conduct appeared to him to be very natural, although, no doubt, it was mistaken. He remarked that when the eyes were first opened to see the beauty, and the heart awakened to feel the purity, of Christianity, it was impossible not to be deeply and painfully struck, almost to disgust, with the glaring discrepancy which the face of the world presented; the whole frame and spirit of society being habitually opposed to many of the requirements of the Gospel, even at this day, and in a world called Christian. During the last few months of his life, he often lamented the trifling and useless manner in which he was constrained to spend a part (sometimes a considerable part) of every day in the numerous visits of inquiry which were made him, and in which the conversation seldom rose above the common topics and news of the day. This was so exceedingly irksome to him as to produce at times some irritation. It was at last suggested to him, that the time so spent might be improved, by turning such visits into an exercise of patience. He was very much pleased with this suggestion, and never after complained of such interruptions, but bore them with great meekness and patience.

Another brief passage from one of his letters written about this time, although both his strength and his sight were then so much impaired as to make writing very difficult to him, is so expressive of his happy frame of mind, that it may perhaps fitly be added to save what has just been said from the misconception to which it might possibly expose such a complaint. " Mr. ―――― a pious young preacher with whom we have been blessed since Christmas, and whose sermons I have been delighted with, and who often calls to see me, expressed his surprise that, in these circumstances, I was always so cheerful. But I told him I never was happier, nay so happy, in my life, surrounded with every comfort, with little real suffering, and with the blessed assurance of a renewed and sanctified heart, which carries with it a conviction so strong of being made an heir to the promise of eternal happiness. Methinks indeed that this internal experience of a total change of the creature, which is as clear as that of our existence, is the most decisive evidence of the truth of holy writ. How should we adore that Holy and Merciful Being who has called us to it!"

But, however premature his removal from the scene of active usefulness might appear, he had already done much, and that not only for his contemporaries, but for the durable benefit of his profession and of mankind. He was a sound scholar and an accomplished physician, wanting nothing to adorn and complete the character proper to his rank. He loved learning for its own sake. Science was to him as his daily food; and the exercise of his art, whether in private or in public, was in the strictest sense professional, so as to exhibit altogether, with such qualifications, a character of great value in itself, and much interest to all who have the good of the medical profession at heart. The course of education, the method of study, and the habits by which such a reputation was attained, and which led to so much of public usefulness, cannot be unimportant, either to the young who are entering upon the same path, or to those who are responsible for their instruction. The effect of what is directly taught, and also of that large and indefinite influence which is flowing in on all sides upon the mind from indirect sources, begins much earlier than is sometimes supposed. Whatever could throw any light on this most important part of the subject has been here related. Nothing, in fine, has been kept back, through the knowledge of which any good to others might be hoped for. The purpose in view, with whatsoever affection and partiality it has been accompanied, is not so much to develope the excellencies of the character, as to set it in its integrity before those who may better justify that high estimate of the value of his labours, which was universally awarded to Dr. BATEMAN while he lived; and to make known to the world those steps by which so unwearied a student, and so zealous and enlightened a physician, so successfully pursued his objects. The testimonies of the familiar friends and companions of his studies were warm and earnest. " If sterling moral worth during life be entitled to praise," were the words of one whom he regarded with particular esteem, " and religious hope in the hour of death be desirable; if high professional repute, and personal estimation be honourable distinctions among men; if warm affections and steady friendship claim and justify attachment, then is his character to be held in respect, and his memory to be long and dearly cherished."

" The more I knew Dr. BATEMAN, the more did I respect him for his integrity and his understanding," was the brief but expressive tribute of another distinguished physician in the metropolis. And " in him," wrote a third, whose eminent place in the public estimation it is earnestly to be hoped that science and humanity will long benefit by, " in him we have lost more perspicuity, judgment, greater extent of learning, and more practical familiarity with disease, than are combined in any other man whom I have ever known."

Equally honourable to his character is the language of affectionate recollection in which his name is mentioned, in conjunction with that of the late truly estimable Dr. EDWARD PERCIVAL, by an intelligent writer in the Edinburgh Medical and Surgical Journal. " Dr. BATEMAN and Dr. PERCIVAL are now both insensible to praise and censure. Of the latter, indeed, they received no portion during their lives; and the former may now be more freely bestowed upon them that it cannot offend their delicacy. To say that we enjoyed their friendship, is to praise ourselves; that we deeply lament their loss, is to express the opinion of the whole profession." The able article (Review of Works on the Epidemic Fever, No. LXIX. p. 631.) from which this last passage is extracted, presents internal evidence of having proceeded from the pen of the highly distinguished editor of that work; and may be considered therefore as dictated equally by public and private feeling.

Such evidences that Dr. BATEMAN had won the esteem of his contemporaries, as well as the affection of his personal friends, were multiplied in the expressions of regard uniformly entertained for him, and as unequivocally manifested by the deep interest and regret excited by his protracted illness and early death.

How amply he merited such attachment, and how justly his conduct in life was entitled to eulogium, these pages would bear witness; not without a natural solicitude for his honour, but chiefly for the sake of the lesson which may be drawn from them for the benefit of those who are engaged in similar occupations; and still more of such as are entering upon their medical education. The particular services which he rendered to his own period, and to posterity, as a physician zealous and successful in the discharge of varied and arduous duties, and as an able and instructive writer, may encourage both, as the best tokens of reward, not to be gained indeed without the same high estimate of the value of time, and the indefatigable assiduity which was its result; but, *with them*, to be hoped for by all who endeavour as conscientiously as he did to qualify themselves for the public confidence.

The details of the methods by which success in one profession has been attained, include so many particulars which may be applied to the prosecution of it in any other, that as it is easy to separate them from what is only technical, they have here been given with a view to general usefulness. And the same object has been still more anxiously sought in the account of that happy acknowledgement of religious truth, with which his earthly course concluded; not for the sake only of relating the remarkable circumstances of that great change, but of recording also the importance of an early care of religious instruction. The pleasing effects of such an education were sufficiently observable through the childhood and the youth of the subject of this memoir. And perhaps more than one of his surviving friends may remember with what earnestness he would argue against the scepticism which first disturbed him; and with what delight he would fly to discourse not likely to offend him with it. Neither probably was it without a strong sense of the principles and emotions of the days he spent under those very respectable men, that, on completing his academical studies, he dedicated their first fruits to his schoolmasters; and that he confined his doubts so much within his own breast, as very rarely to speak of them but with a direct view to sober discussion; and had, so long after, formed an intention of examining into the evidences of Revelation. But whatever might be the secret influences of his early religious education; whether these were of so much importance or not, in modifying the frame of his mind during the active portion of his life, and in preparing it for that comfort to which it was ultimately recalled, the positive evidences of their value is sufficient to encourage an earnest perseverance in all the practices calculated to implant and confirm them in childhood. He had scarcely, indeed, completed his honourable career through the schools, when his early religious impressions underwent a change which, in no long time, settled into indifference, and afterwards into unbelief. In this frame his mind continued throughout his active and very useful professional life; in his morals still, as he always had been, virtuous, but unconvinced of the truth of the Christian Revelation. He left London with the intention of returning in a few weeks; but in this purpose he was disappointed. The end, as it proved, was set to his connections with this world; but, like a dawning light, views, to which he had long been a stranger, gradually returned upon him. In the most satisfactory and most comfortable sense his conversion was complete. It was a conversion, not to a philosophical persuasion that there *may be* a life to come, but to a solemn and happy possession of his whole heart and soul with the truths and promises of the Gospel. His faculties were never clearer, never stronger; and to all who were acquainted with the sincerity and the singular sobriety of his character, his example must be inexpressibly striking. Science had in every way so well repaid his diligence, that it would not perhaps be easy to produce an instance of a person better qualified to appreciate its benefits. His mind, long chastened to the strictness which science demands, retained its best characteristics; and no one could be more keenly alive to the worldly advantages which his high attainments procured for him; or could feel more painfully the interruption of fair prospects, or rather, of the actual enjoyment of eminence. Yet he lived, not to undervalue these things, but to see their value in a light totally different from that which had governed the most considerable portion of his days: for he now regarded them as valuable, only as they were useful to others; and with a higher sense therefore of their worth, as well as of their obligations, gave impressive proof of the sufficiency of Christain principles for all vicissitudes, in " that peace and joy in believing" with which he contemplated his approaching separation from all earthly connections. After many months so spent, his last hours were most affecting. As fully in possession of himself as at any part of his life, he perceived his dissolution to be at hand; and, with expressions of a primitive simplicity and resignation, expired in the assured and most comfortable hope of a blissful immortality!

Thus, finally, to conclude the duty of these pages, and to part justly, though reluctantly, with their subject, worthy as it is of a far more extended illustration, Dr. BATEMAN's youth was happy, his life virtuous and useful, and his death blessed. It is not for us to inquire farther into the means by which it pleased God so to order his course. Its outward circumstances were not common; but they are easily told; and there was nothing in his conduct, worthy of being followed, which may not be imitated. Of its inward processes, and the impulses by which it was moved, it becomes us to speak only in the language of humility and reverence. His knowledge was various and complete; his humanity always active; his love of truth, moral as well as philosophical, remarkable throughout his history. These are within the comprehension of all; and to do less than seek an equal advancement in whatsoever belongs to our own duties, will be to incur, be our outward success for a time what it may, a reproach from conscience, which can never be put to rest. With a like care to obey that conscience, from its earliest dictates to its latest, life may be in like manner crowned with usefulness and honour; and death may be met with the same peace, and thankfulness, and hope, and joy!

THE END.

LONDON:
Printed by A. & R. Spottiswoode,
New-Street-Square.

Check Out More Titles From HardPress Classics Series In this collection we are offering thousands of classic and hard to find books. This series spans a vast array of subjects – so you are bound to find something of interest to enjoy reading and learning about.

Subjects:
Architecture
Art
Biography & Autobiography
Body, Mind &Spirit
Children & Young Adult
Dramas
Education
Fiction
History
Language Arts & Disciplines
Law
Literary Collections
Music
Poetry
Psychology
Science
…and many more.

Visit us at www.hardpress.net

Im The Story
personalised classic books

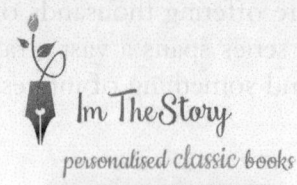

"Beautiful gift.. lovely finish. My Niece loves it, so precious!"

Helen R Brumfieldon

★★★★★

JANE IN WONDERLAND
LEWIS CARROLL

UNIQUE GIFT
FOR KIDS, PARTNERS AND FRIENDS

Timeless books such as:

Kids

Alice in Wonderland • The Jungle Book • The Wonderful Wizard of Oz
Peter and Wendy • Robin Hood • The Prince and The Pauper
The Railway Children • Treasure Island • A Christmas Carol

Adults

Romeo and Juliet • Dracula

- **Highly** Customizable
- **Change** Books Title
- **Replace** Characters Names with yours
- **Upload** Photo for inside page
- **Add** Inscriptions

Visit **ImTheStory.com**
and order yours today!

WS - #0176 - 130125 - C0 - 229/152/14 - PB - 9780461680690 - Gloss Lamination